GUITAR *signature licks*

THE BEST OF
DJANGO REINHARDT

A STEP-BY-STEP BREAKDOWN OF THE GUITAR STYLES AND TECHNIQUES OF A JAZZ GIANT

W0006982

CW00797162

by Joe Charupakorn

Cover photo from The Frank Driggs Collection

ISBN 0-634-03431-6

HAL•LEONARD®
CORPORATION
7777 W. BLUEMOUND RD. P.O. BOX 13819 MILWAUKEE, WI 53213

Visit Hal Leonard Online at
www.halleonard.com

CONTENTS

INTRODUCTION

Just about a half century after his death, Django Reinhardt still remains a towering figure in the annals of jazz guitar. To this day, his incendiary playing stands up to that of later virtuoso jazz guitarists such as Joe Pass, Pat Martino, and George Benson. Author James Lincoln Collier, in his book *The Making of Jazz*, calls Django "the most important guitarist in the history of jazz"; when you take into account the hordes of jazz guitarists he has influenced, he may very well be. His groundbreaking style of playing—marrying European-influenced scales and harmonies with jazz rhythms—was unheard of during his time. He was among the first of the European jazz musicians who could cop the jazz feel correctly, and he left an indelible stamp on the world of jazz guitar. His major influence was session guitarist Eddie Lang (the first major jazz guitarist). He absorbed Lang's European-based harmonic concepts and took them one step beyond.

Born Jean Baptise Reinhardt to LaBelle Reinhardt and Jean Vées (his assumed father) on January 23, 1910 in Liverchees, Belgium near the French border, Django was raised in true gypsy fashion, travelling around in a caravan and living like a vagabond. He spent much of his formative years travelling across Europe, eventually settling just outside of Paris.

Django did not attend school and was illiterate—he could neither read nor write. He did, however, have a passion and a gift for music and eventually received a banjo from a neighbor named Raclot when he was twelve. He never took formal lessons, but learned from his father and other musicians in the area, and shortly thereafter began playing with his father in cafes. By age fourteen he had become a fixture on the Parisian club scene, and by age eighteen he recorded his first session as a sideman, accompanying an accordion on banjo.

On November 2, 1928, tragedy struck. Django heard some noise and thought it was a rat scurrying around his wagon. He grabbed a candle, which unexpectedly fell out of the candleholder and onto a pile of highly flammable artificial flowers that immediately burst into flames, setting the wagon on fire. Django used a blanket to carry his wife out of the burning caravan, but his exposed legs and left hand were severely burned. Because of the severity of the burn, doctors suggested amputating Django's legs, but he vehemently refused. He would later regain the use of both legs.

His left hand did not have the same good fortune, and his music career appeared to be doomed. Django was resilient, however, and trudged along, trying to play guitar again while in the hospital. He eventually regained the use of his thumb, index, and middle fingers, but never the full use of the ring and pinky fingers. Over a year later, he was able to play again using his functioning left-hand fingers.

In 1928 Django met Stephane Grapelli, a violinist with whom he would have a career-long relationship. They were both struggling young musicians trying to make their way in the jazz scene. In 1933, they finally had the chance to play together in the Quintet of the Hot Club of France (which also featured Django's brother Joseph on rhythm guitar), an incarnation of the Hotel Claridge Orchestra. The Ultraphone Record Company gave the group a record deal in 1934, and their first recording sent shockwaves throughout the European jazz scene. This spawned a series of group recordings that would elevate the group's popularity and allow them to play concert halls.

When World War II started, the group was on tour in London. Django and company retreated to Paris, but Grapelli chose to stay behind in London. As a result of the German invasion of France, Django became a god in the eyes of the French. He was a national hero who represented a unique and free spirit that stood tall against the repressive, stifling nature of the German invaders.

Django's star continued to rise. He composed the beautiful song "Nuages," which would become his signature song, and eventually replaced Grapelli with clarinetist Hubert Rostaing, inspired by the pairing of Charlie Christian and Benny Goodman. This new line-up also had drums replacing rhythm guitar, and would sell out shows wherever it played. Django's popularity spread to include America.

In 1946, Django reunited with Stephane Grapelli. They went on to record as a quintet with new members, but Django was in poor health and returned to Paris. Later in 1946 he made his first and only trip to the United States. He was invited to New York's prestigious Carnegie Hall to be a featured soloist with the Duke Ellington Orchestra. He was excited to come to America, and his tremendous ego gave him severe delusions of grandeur. He left his Maccaferri guitar at home, expecting American guitar makers to swarm him with free guitars to choose from. This did not happen, and he ended up buying a generic American electric that was not quite comfortable for him.

Django pulled off the first concert without a hitch and was asked back for six encores. On the second night, however, in his typical capricious fashion, he showed up late, arriving just in time to close the show; he blamed his tardiness on the cab driver. This event dropped Django's marquee value significantly, and the tour was considered a major flop.

Bebop had become the fashionable style of jazz by 1949, and Django's swing style was passé. His ego was crushed, and he stopped playing guitar for a while. By 1951, however, he was back in action and had assimilated the bebop language. He could bop with the best and was now playing an amplified guitar. He recorded with bebop pioneer Dizzy Gillespie (John Birks) in 1953 and had a world tour lined up.

In Switzerland, on a small tour, Django developed some health problems. He had severe headaches, high blood pressure, and numbness in his fingers. He refused to see a doctor and on May 15, 1953, he suffered a fatal stroke while at a cafe with friends. He died at the young age of 43.

The legend of Django Reinhardt continues to grow. Prominent jazz guitarist Bireli LaGrene devotes himself to carrying the torch Django left behind. Django's influence is immediately evident in LaGrene's playing in his use of tremolo picking, quick chromatic lines, and slides across the fretboard. In 1999, Woody Allen wrote and directed "Sweet and Lowdown," a fictional movie in which a character named Emmet Ray claimed to be "the second greatest jazz guitarist in the world"—second only to Django Reinhardt. Ray was threatened and traumatized by Django's presence and avoided him at all costs. In 2002, a restaurant named "Django," inspired by the Manouche guitarist, opened to critical acclaim in New York City's highly competitive restaurant scene.

DISCOGRAPHY

The songs on the accompanying audio CD are based on the following recordings:

"Dinah"—*Djangology*
"Tiger Rag (Hold That Tiger)"—*Djangology*
"Old Folks at Home (Swanee River)"—*Very Best of Django Reinhardt*
"Djangology"—*Djangology*
"Limehouse Blues"—*Djangology*
"Stardust"—*Very Best of Django Reinhardt*
"Swing Guitar"—*Djangology*
"Ain't Misbehavin' "—*Djangology*
"Rose Room"—*Djangology*
"Minor Swing"—*Best of Django Reinhardt*
"Daphne"—*Djangology*
"Nuages"—*Djangology*
"Swing 42"—*Djangology*
"Belleville"—*Djangology*
"Honeysuckle Rose"—*Swing Guitar*
"Marie"—*Djangology 49*

THE RECORDING

Doug Boduch	Guitar
Joseph Ketchum	Violin
Warren Wiegratz	Clarinet
Tom McGirr	Bass
Scott Schroedl	Drums

Recorded, mixed, and mastered by Jim Reith at Beathouse Music, Milwaukee, WI

ABOUT THE AUTHOR

Joe Charupakorn is a guitarist, composer, author, and editor who has written and edited over a dozen books, including the four-volume internationally acclaimed *Guitar Reference Guides* series, published by Cherry Lane Music. He currently resides in New York City's East Village. Visit him on the web at www.joecharupakorn.com

DINAH

Words by Sam M. Lewis and Joe Young
Music by Harry Akst

Figure 1—Solo

"Dinah" was the first song Django recorded with the Quintet of the Hot Club of France, the group that teamed him up with violinist Stephane Grapelli. Django's association with Grapelli, inspired by their predecessors Eddie Lang and Joe Venuti and their jazz guitar/violin duo, would continue for a large part of his career.

The solo on "Dinah" makes prominent use of tremolo picking, one of Django's favorite techniques. Tremolo picking uses the right hand to continuously pick as fast as possible. There are two kinds of tremolo picking generally recognized: *measured and unmeasured*. With measured tremolo, you can perceive an exact subdivision of the beat; with unmeasured tremolo, you hear the notes go by as fast as possible with no specific subdivision. Starting in measure 7, Django tremolo picks a triplet pattern that consists of a note followed by a neighbor note a half step above and then back to the original note. This pattern is sequenced down in half steps from F♯ to F♯ an octave lower. After the lower F♯ is reached, Django tremolo picks a series of both fretted and open-string notes. The phrase culminates in a unison of fretted and open-string notes in measures 13–15.

2 Full Band

3 Slow Demo
Gtr. 1 meas. 1-17

Fig. 1

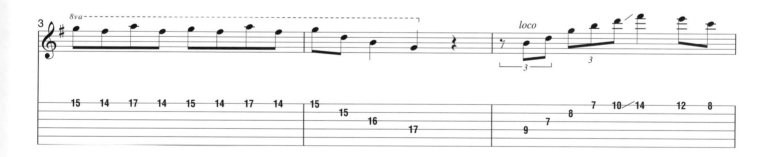

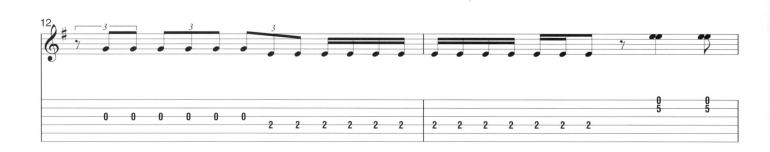

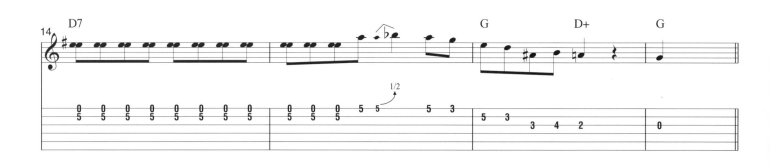

TIGER RAG (HOLD THAT TIGER)

Words by Harry DeCosta
Music by Original Dixieland Jazz Band

Figure 2–Head

This scorching tour de force will give even the most advanced pickers a challenge. The tune is played super uptempo, at 320 beats per minute, and has continuous motion by way of Django's accurate, ascending and descending scalar passages in eighth notes. Even jazz guitar monster Pat Martino would have to practice this head!

The violin (here transcribed for guitar) primarily doubles the guitar a 6th higher until the B section (measures 17–24), where the violin plays a melody in half- and quarter-note rhythms and the guitar comps in a similar manner. In measures 25–32, the lightning-fast scale lines return.

At measure 33 there is a key change to E♭, a 4th higher than the original key of B♭. This section has two breaks that allow Django to fill in the spaces with outpouring streams of notes. For the run in measures 35–37, he takes a shape of three chromatically ascending notes and moves it down string-by-string from the high E string to the A string. Since this is a pattern of three eighth notes against a 4/4 meter, a three-against-four hemiola is created. A *hemiola* occurs when a simple meter is superimposed over a compound meter or vice versa.

The next unaccompanied run heard in measures 39–41 is derived from the B♭ Mixolydian mode (B♭–C–D–E♭–F–G–A♭). This line outlines the dominant chord (B♭7) using functional chromaticism to create motion. Notice how Django integrates open strings into the line.

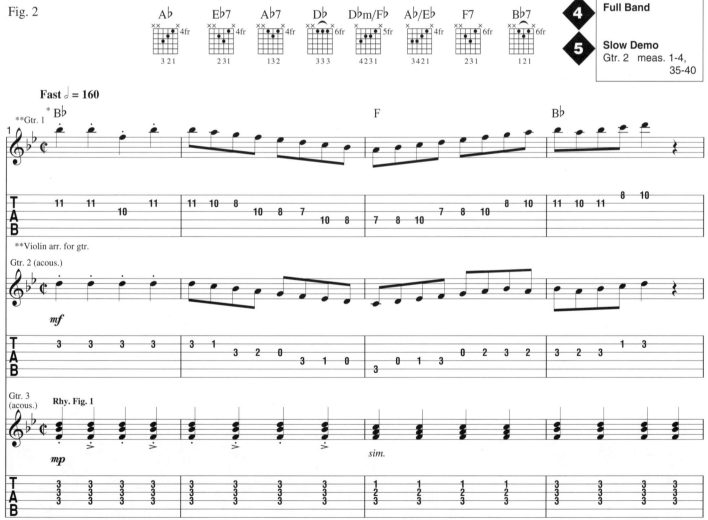

*Chord symbols reflect overall harmony.

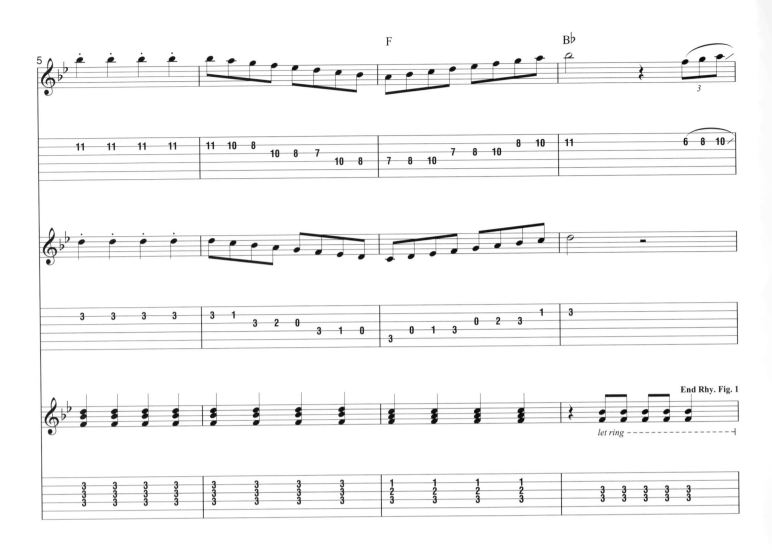

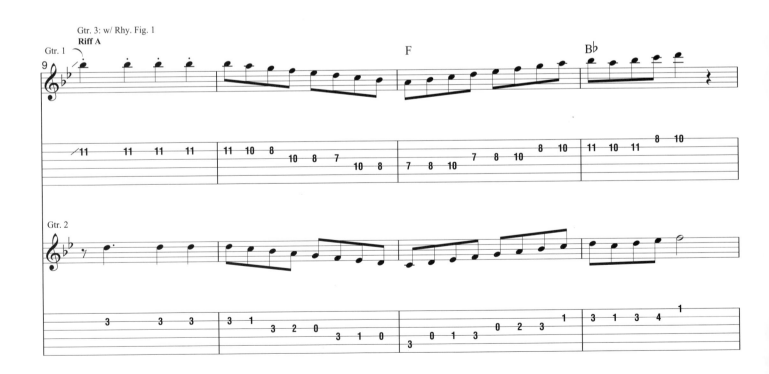

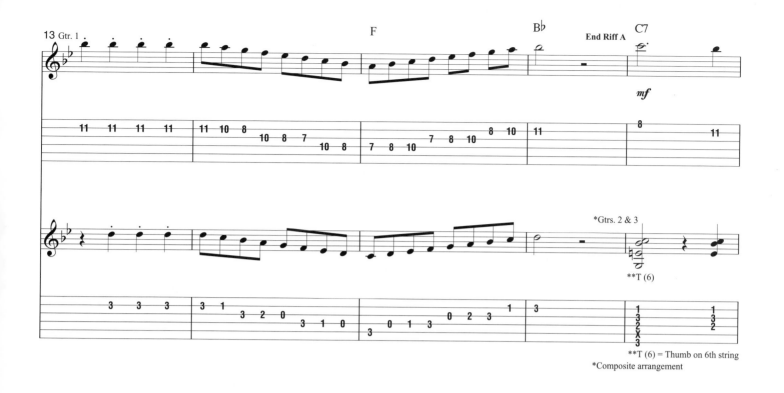

**T (6) = Thumb on 6th string
*Composite arrangement

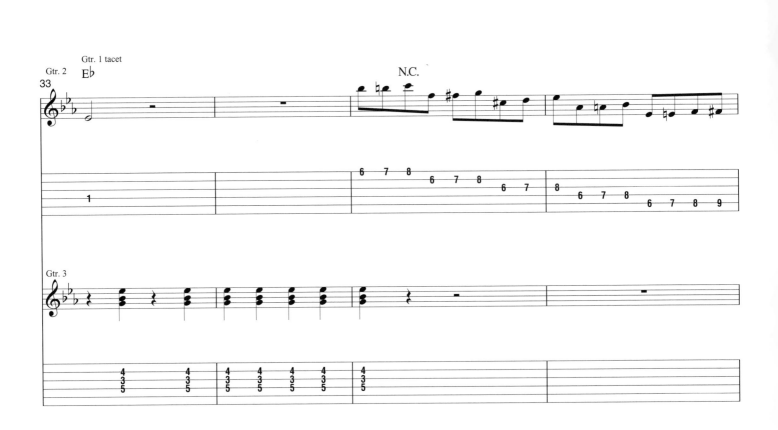

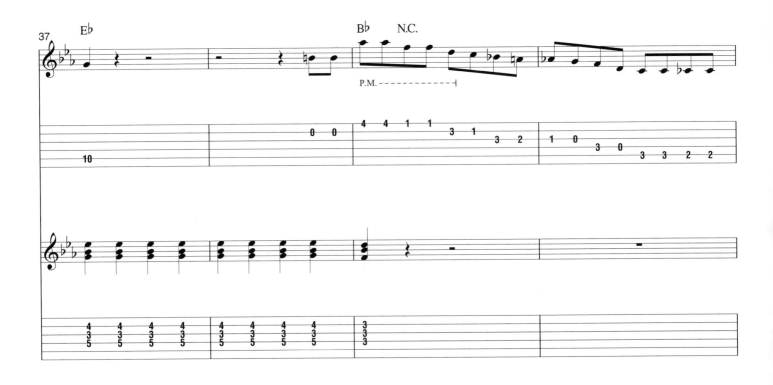

*T (5 & 6) = Thumb on 5th & 6th strings

Figure 3 – Solo

Now in A♭ (a 4th higher than the previous key, E♭), the solo section starts off with a different feel created by Django's minimalist approach. For the first eight measures, he employs lyrical bends in half and whole notes to contrast against the underlying fast pulse. Here, Django sounds very relaxed as he bends into chord notes, until measure 9 when he whips out a quick scale run.

Rather than continuing to burn up and down the fretboard as one might expect, Django takes a motivic approach in measures 12–17, starting with a melody of E♭–B–C. The next repetition of this fragment uses E instead of E♭, while the other two notes (B–C) are the same. The final repetition goes back to E♭ and then develops into a bending-infused melody that resolves to the tonic (A♭).

The repeated Fm7 arpeggio in measures 18–20 leads into a tremolo-picked (see "Dinah") high A♭ that is sustained through the chord change from A♭ to D♭. In measures 25–26, Django introduces a repetitive melody in quarter notes that evolves into the quarter-note triplet lick in measures 27–28. This lick uses a two-beat pattern descending in 3rds against a triplet rhythm resulting in a two-against-three hemiola.

Fig. 3

| **6** | **Full Band** |
| **7** | **Slow Demo** Gtr. 2 meas. 1-32 |

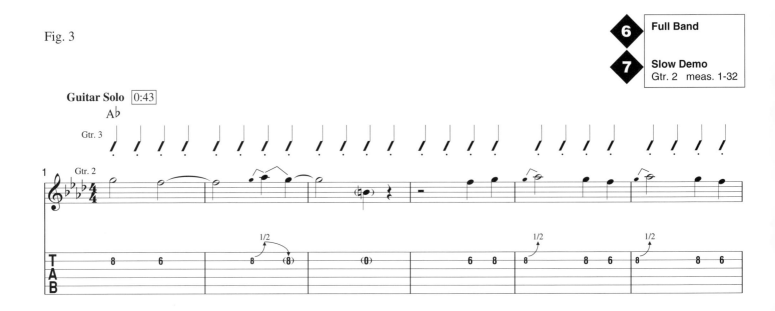

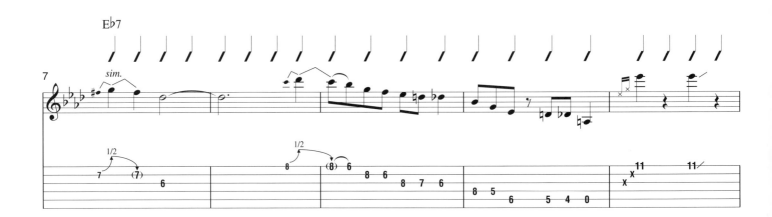

OLD FOLKS AT HOME (SWANEE RIVER)

Words and Music by Stephen C. Foster

Figure 4–Intro and Head

"Old Folks at Home (Swanee River)," the state song of Florida, was written by Stephen Foster about the river that extends from the Okeefenokee Swamp in Georgia to the Gulf of Mexico in Florida. Here, Django and partner-in-crime Stephane Grapelli tear it up with their killer rendition, transforming a joyous state song into a vehicle for their virtuosity.

"Old Folks at Home" starts off with a simple melody played in octaves and harmonized with dyads (played by Gtr.2). The underlying harmony is C+7, which is derived from the C whole tone scale (C–D–E–F♯–G♯–B♭), the dominant of F (the key of the head). Using this scale evokes a mysterious mood that adds to the color of the intro. As the sound of this scale is very distinctive, moderate use of this scale is the best approach to prevent predictability—Django only exploits this tonality for four-measure segments here.

In the head to "Old Folks at Home," Grapelli plays the melody (here arranged for guitar) while Django comps away, providing rock-solid support. Django uses the "boom-chick" pattern of bass note followed by chord to keep the tempo steady, as there are no drums. The chords are four-note voicings primarily played on the inner strings.

The violin melody is all in fifth position on guitar, so it should be fairly easy to play. The tricky aspect of the melody is in the rhythm—quarter- and half-note triplets abound. The best approach to catching these rhythms is to first listen to the accompanying CD, then try and duplicate the rhythms by ear as accurately as possible. Doing this will also help you internalize the sound of these rhythms.

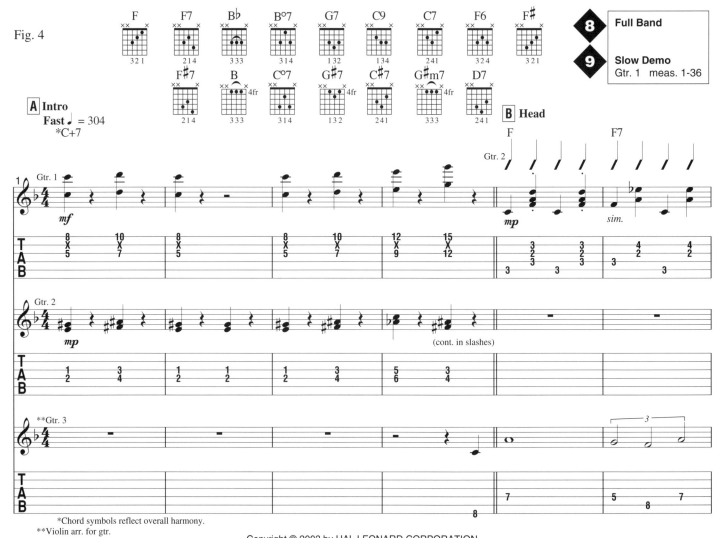

*Chord symbols reflect overall harmony.
**Violin arr. for gtr.

Figure 5–Solo and Interlude

With a modulation up a half step from the key of F to F♯, Django starts right off the bat with his long, blistering lines at a very fast tempo (304 beats per minute). This solo is one of his most burning recorded moments, even more astounding considering that Django is only using two fingers to fret the notes. The lines consist primarily of scalar and arpeggio passages based on the F♯ major scale (F♯–G♯–A♯–B–C♯–D♯–E♯) with the ♭3rd (A♮) used occasionally. In measures 5–8, check out how Django uses arpeggios to elicit a rising sound. Each successive arpeggio ends on a higher note culminating on a trill that starts on a high A. In measures 13–16 a similar arpeggio run is heard.

In measure 9 Django plays a simple motive—C♯ to A♯ alternating in a quarter-note/quarter-note rest rhythm. This motive is developed over the next three measures using a rhythmic approach. While only two notes are used, the rhythm keeps the line active with syncopation in measure 10, diminution in measure 11, and eighth notes in measure 12.

The different sections of this tune are marked by a modulation to the key a half step higher. This interlude is in the key of G, one half step up from F♯ (the solo key), and is comprised of the transposed melody to "Old Folks at Home" doubled in octaves. The octaves give the melody a more pronounced sound and reinforce the strength of the melody. The interlude winds down with chords in measures 63–64.

Fig. 5

10 Full Band

11 Slow Demo
Gtr. 1 meas. 1-32

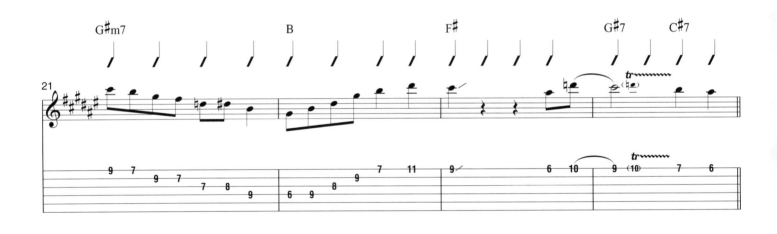

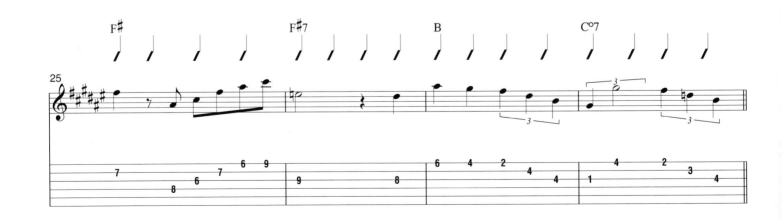

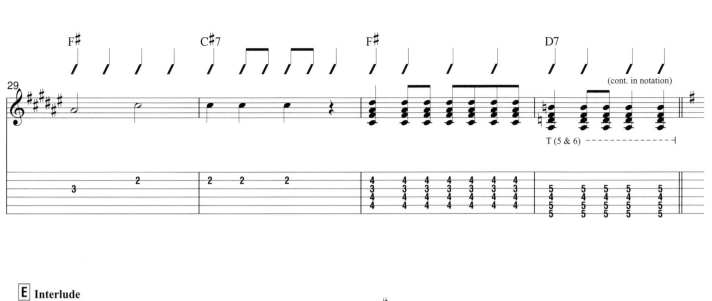

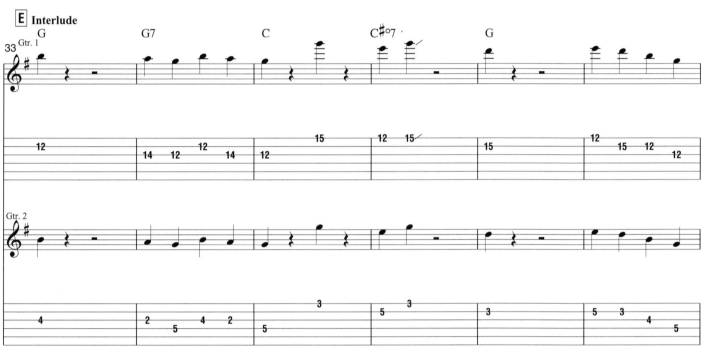

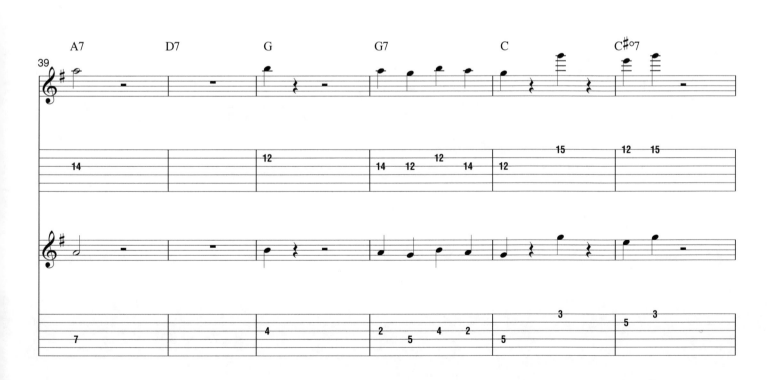

DJANGOLOGY
By Django Reinhardt and Stephane Grapelli

Figure 6–Intro

"Djangology" starts off with the guitar and violin (here transcribed for guitar) harmonized and outlining the chord changes. Arpeggio-based figures are used to traverse the fretboard and create a wide-range sound. These figures are played in a continuous triplet rhythm.

While the guitar and violin move in similar motion, they are not harmonized in a conventional sense (parallel 3rds, 6ths, or octaves), resulting in a potpourri of harmonies. The reason this approach works here is that the guitar and violin are both sticking primarily to chord tones, which are the unifying factor. Although the harmonies themselves don't follow an obvious pattern, the sound of each chord is heard clearly from the individual lines.

Fig. 6

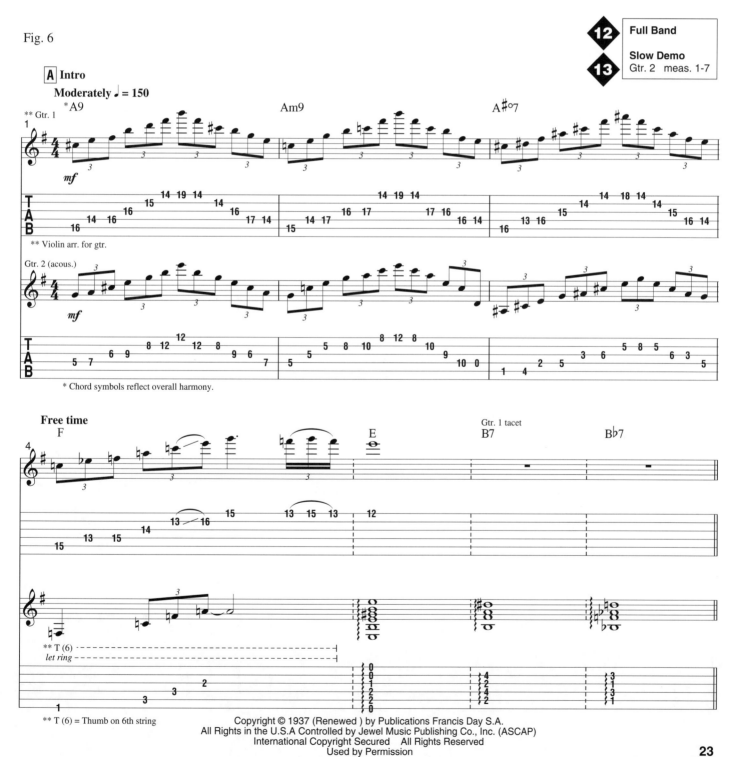

* Chord symbols reflect overall harmony.

** T (6) = Thumb on 6th string

Figure 7–Head

The head is comprised of an unusual twenty-eight-measure AABA form, with the B section consisting of only four measures. The buoyancy of the head contrasts nicely with the intro's technical character. The opening measures of the head resemble the intro in both melodic and harmonic content with the melody based on arpeggios. These arpeggio shapes are played from the third to the first string. Similar arpeggios are heard in measures 9–10, 18, and 21.

In measures 7–9 a riff based on G minor is displaced on each recurrence. This shifts the perception of the downbeat and produces a hypnotic effect against the quarter-note pulse. Notice that the G minor riff is played over a G chord. A bluesy effect is created from the use of the minor 3rd (B♭) over a major chord.

Django's comping in straight quarter notes serves as a rhythmic anchor similar to that of Freddie Green (the late guitarist of the Count Basie Orchestra), who is famous for this style of comping. The chord voicings Django uses are based on barre chord forms. He sounds the chord notes on the upper strings while skipping over the lower strings to achieve a lean, flowing sound.

Fig. 7

14 | **Full Band**

15 | **Slow Demo** / Gtr. 2 meas. 1-28

24

Figure 8 – Solo

Django's one-chorus solo crams an assortment of guitar techniques into a nifty little package. Here he pulls out all the stops, tearing up the fretboard as if there's no tomorrow. In measures 5–8 he uses slides to create a liquid feel, adding vibrato to the last note to add finality to the phrase.

The run in measure 4 is influenced by a similar run used over the same chord in the head. Django starts the phrase by employing a quick trill from a note to its upper neighbor and back. This is followed by an arpeggiated descent, which leads into an ascending arpeggio. This strategy is employed throughout the solo whenever a C#°7 chord is sounded, as in measures 12 and 24.

Measures 9–10 allude to the intro with its climbing arpeggios. Django fingers the run with a combination of fretted notes and open strings. In measures 16–18, he plays a phrase in octaves, muting the inner string to prevent unwanted string noise. Conventionally, these shapes are played with the index finger and pinky, but Django makes do with his index and middle fingers.

A hemiola occurs in measures 21–22 with each note lasting for a beat and a half. The melody here is made up of a chromatic descent from the 9th (B) of the A7 chord to the root. Over the C minor chord, the ♭7th (B♭) sounded.

Fig. 8

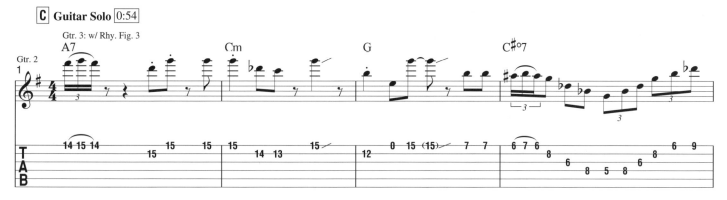

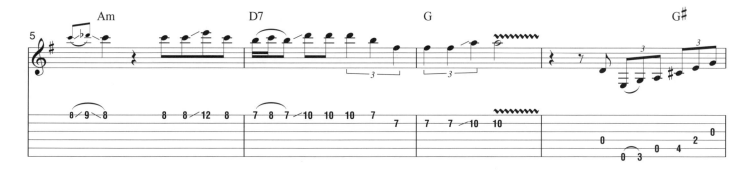

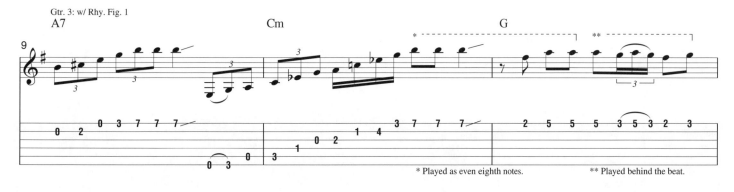

* Played as even eighth notes.   ** Played behind the beat.

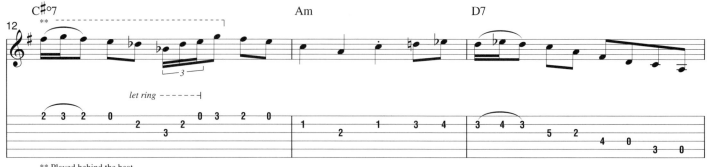

** Played behind the beat.

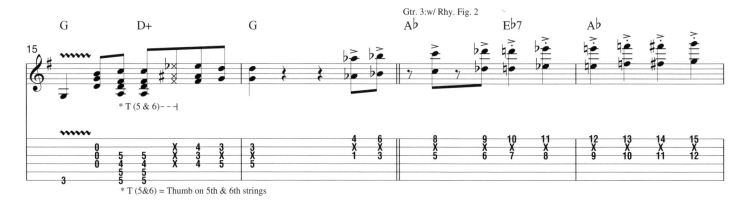

* T (5&6) = Thumb on 5th & 6th strings

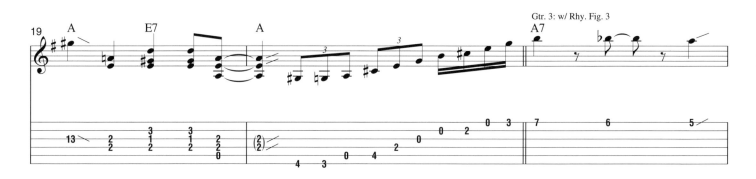

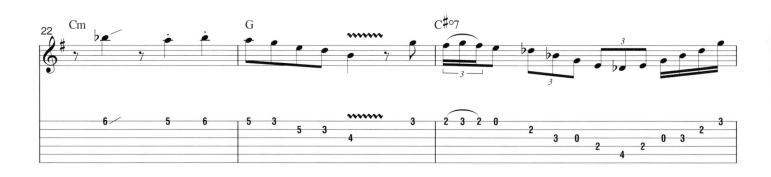

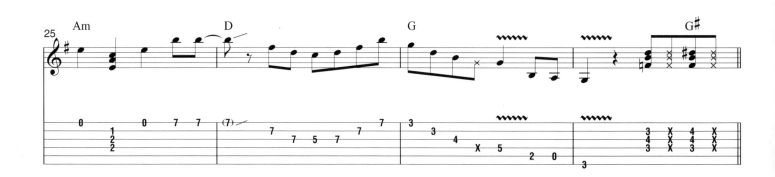

LIMEHOUSE BLUES

Words by Douglas Furber
Music by Phillip Braham

Figure 9–Head

Django is not immediately thought of as a rhythm guitarist—his soloing ability commands all of the attention—but his comping on "Limehouse Blues" can quickly change that perception. At a very fast tempo, Django comps primarily in quarter notes, and the time never falters—even without a drummer. He uses a "boom-chick" pattern with the bass note played on beats 1 and 3 followed by the chord on beats 2 and 4.

The violin melody is transcribed here, arranged for guitar. It is made up of quarter and half notes played over an undulating uptempo pulse. The melody is fairly easy to play since it stays primarily in the fifth position throughout the head. Some out-of-position shifts are played in measures 25–29.

18	Full Band
19	Slow Demo
	Gtr. 3 meas. 1-32, 33-64, 65-96

Fig. 9

* Chords reflect overall harmony.
** Violin arr. for gtr.
*** Gtrs. 2&3 (acous.)
*** Composite arrangement

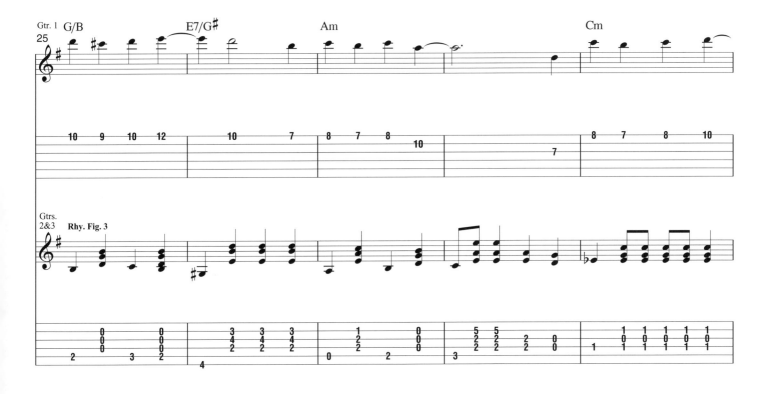

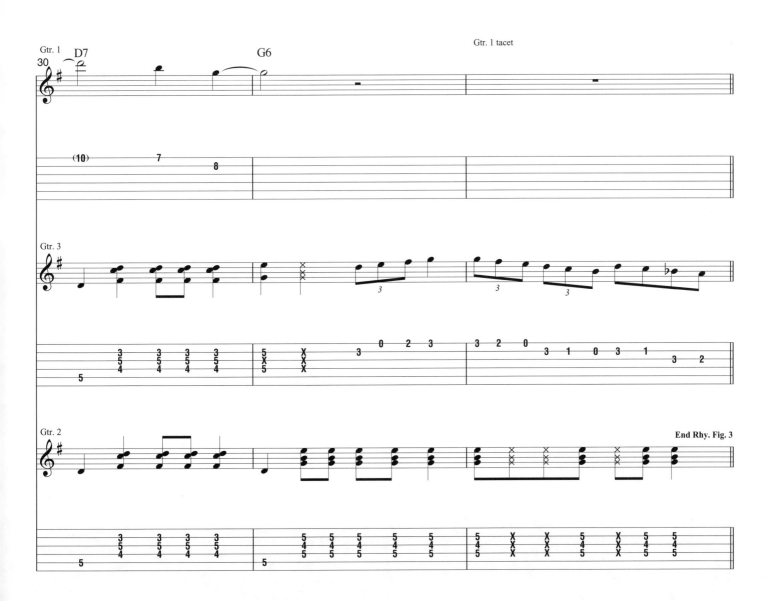

Figure 10–Solo

    Django follows a soloing strategy that Wes Montgomery would later popularize—
lines followed by octaves, then chords. Django starts off with some single-note lines that
outline the changes. Here, he plays in his typical virtuosic manner with long, continuous
strings of eighth notes and triplets. Then octaves are added to the mix, as in measures
9–12, 29–37, 71–73, and 91–95. For a climax, Django builds into a chord solo in measures
77–87. Check out the use of tremolo picking in measures 81–87, which adds a swelling
sound to the chords.

    In this solo, open strings are prominently contrasted with fretted notes to create
tonal coloring. Django alternates the open high E string with the fretted A note in measure
6. In measures 55–57 he uses the high E string as a pedal point against an E Phrygian
(E–F–G–A–B–C–D) line. A cool unison lick comprised of an open B string against a fretted B exploits the contrasting timbre of open and fretted notes in measures 43–46. Here
Django creates a hemiola by accenting the first of every three eighth notes against the 4/4
meter.

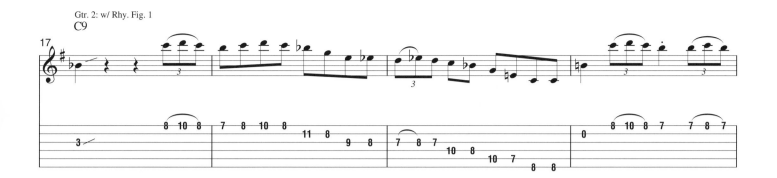

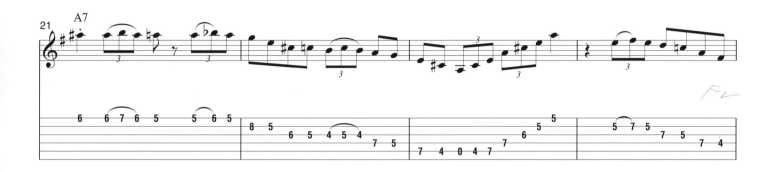

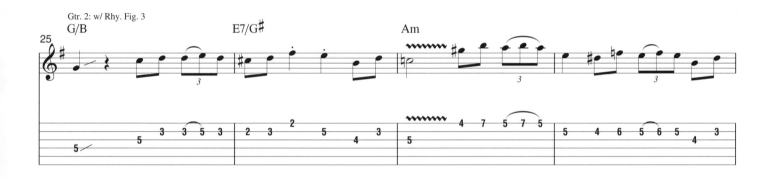

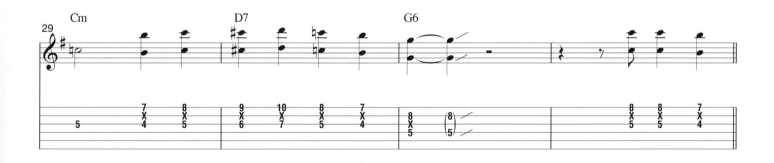

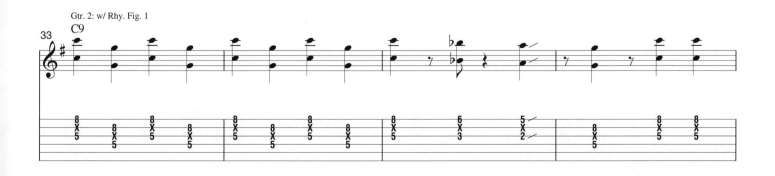

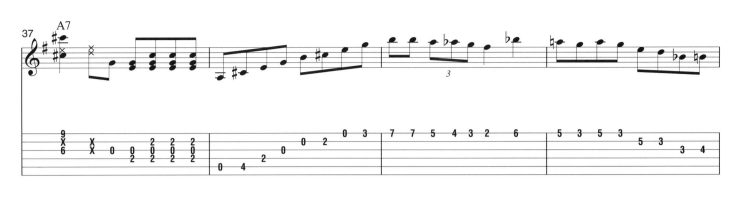

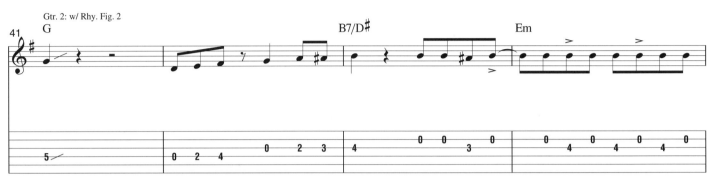

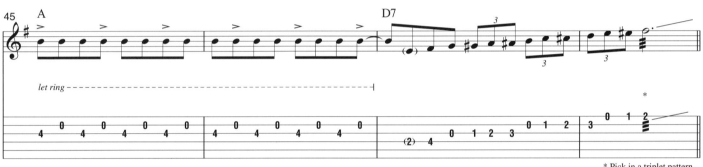

* Pick in a triplet pattern.

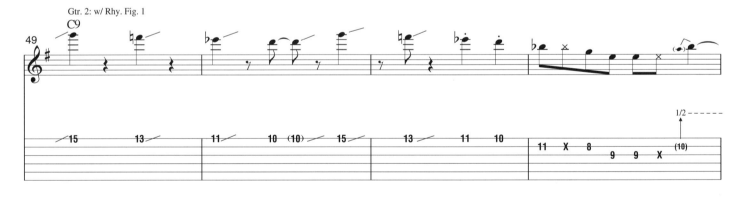

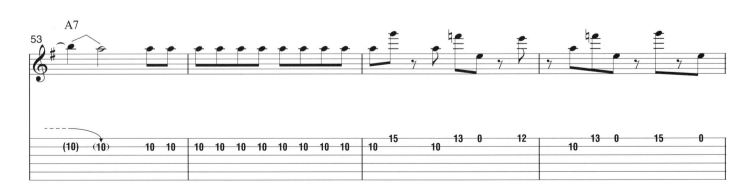

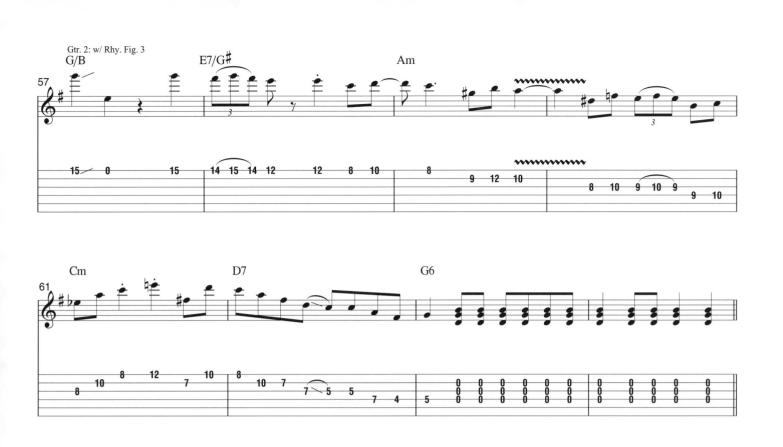

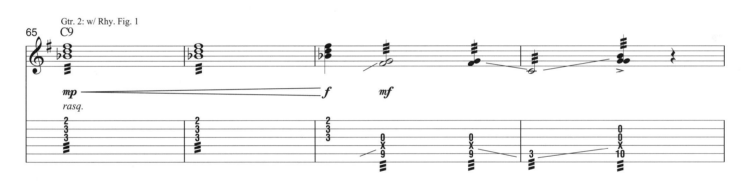

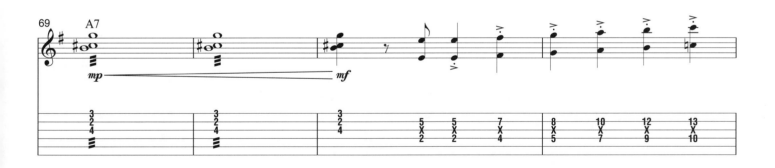

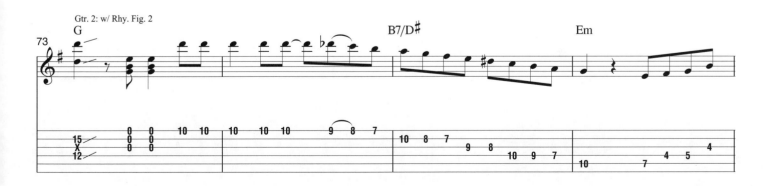

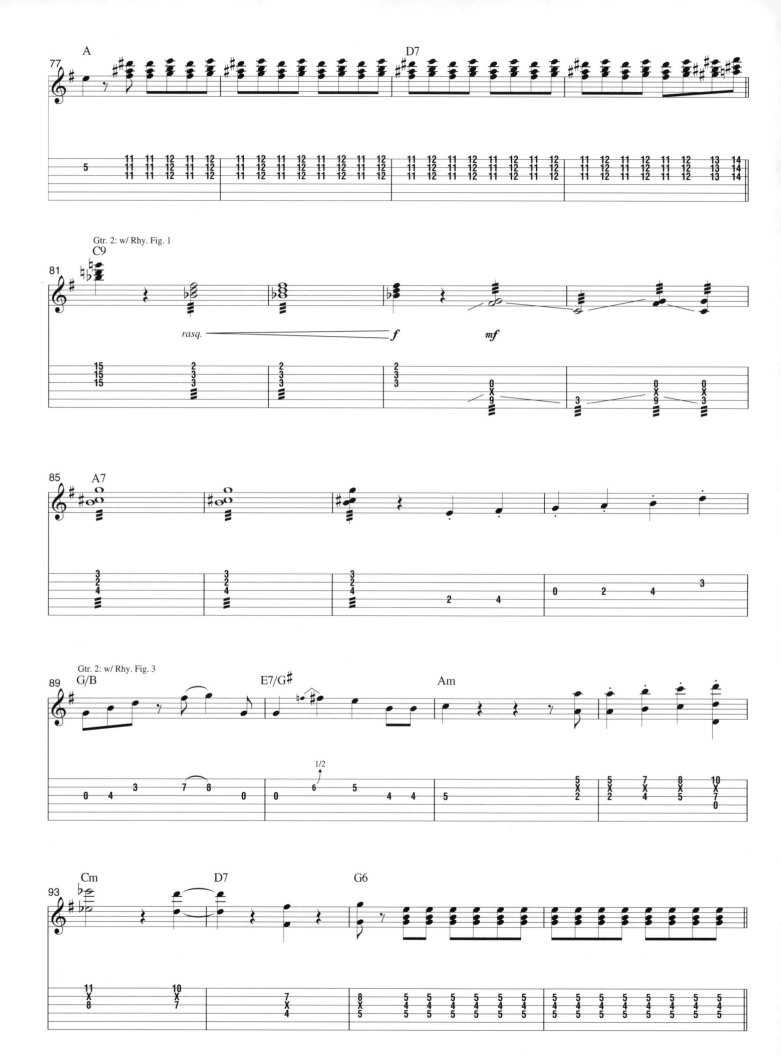

STARDUST

Words by Mitchell Parish
Music by Hoagy Carmichael

Figure 11–Head

The Hoagy Carmichael standard "Stardust" has, over time, earned its place as a true American classic. In this transcription, the piano (arranged for guitar) plays the melody, and the guitar comps along. The head is a thirty-two-measure AABA form, the most common song form in jazz. Learning the piano melody on guitar is helpful for learning how other instrumentalists phrase a melody. Notice that there are some familiar chord/arpeggio shapes used. In measure 1, an E♭m7 arpeggio shape is used to finger the melody, and in measure 6 an F minor triad shape is used over the B♭7 chord. More chord/arpeggio shapes are used in measures 19–20, 28–29, and 31–32.

Django doesn't solo on this version, but his comping offers plenty to examine. Typical of Django's comping style—and the general style of the Swing era—a quarter-note pulse is established by playing chords all on the downbeats. There are no syncopations used by the rhythm section, so the time is always lucid. Syncopations in the melody add a nice rhythmic dissonance when layered on top of this constant pulse. For example, look at the piano melody in the first four measures. Anticipations (arriving at a note sooner than its expected time) are used in measures 1–4 with the last beat of measures 1 and 2 arriving at the target note an eighth note earlier. In measure 3, a syncopated rhythm that accents the upbeat before beats 1, 2, and 3 ensues. The syncopation in measure 4 accents the upbeat before beat 2. All of these syncopations played against Django's steady rhythm create the illusion of shifting beats.

Django primarily works from three-note chord shapes. When he plays a note on the low E string, as in measures 6–7, it is fingered with his thumb. He does it again in measures 13–16, this time fretting notes on the A string as well with his thumb. Similar thumb usage occurs in measures 22–23 and 32. Conventionally, using the thumb to fret notes is a big "no-no" but Django used it out of necessity and produced wonderful results.

Fig. 11

* Chord symbols reflect overall harmony.

*** T(6) = Thumb on 6th string.

*T(5&6)=Thumb on 5th & 6th strings.

SWING GUITAR

By Django Reinhardt and Stephane Grapelli

Figure 12–Head

The head, transcribed here for guitar, is played by the violin. It's written in a standard thirty-two-measure AABA form using a stock progression in the key of C. The melody is fairly diatonic, using chord tones to connect the chords. The ♭3 (E♭) is used sparingly in measures 1 and 6 to evoke a bluesy sound. Chromatic approach tones are used in measure 4 (G♯–A), 11 (D♯–E), 26 and 28 (G♯–A), and 29 (F♯–A–A♭) to smoothly connect target notes.

While the A section is constantly moving, the rhythmic use of only two notes (B and E) in measures 21–23 of the B section provide a brief respite. This leads back into the final A section and then to the solo. Learning the head will give you some cool licks to add to your improvising vocabulary and inspire you to create your own lines.

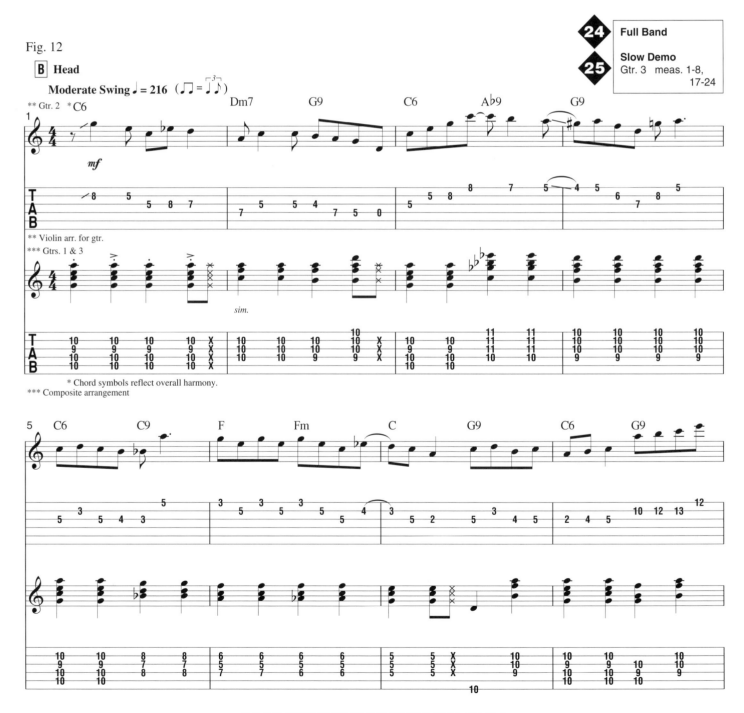

Fig. 12

B Head

Moderate Swing ♩ = 216

* Chord symbols reflect overall harmony.
*** Composite arrangement

Figure 13–Solo

Modulating up a half step from the key of C to D♭, the solo section displays Django's consistent ability to build a solo and keep the intensity going. The solo starts off with a first-inversion D♭ triad played on the upper three strings on the downbeat. This is the only chord he plays in the solo until the final two measures (64 and 65), as the solo is predominantly littered with long lines.

Django's lines include some unifying motivic elements. A triplet motive begins in measures 9–12. This becomes a springboard for the arpeggiated run in measures 12–13. The triplet motive is recalled in measures 42–44. Here, Django resolves the first triplet pattern into a sustained, dissonant ♭9 tone (A) over A♭7. The next triplet resolves into the 3rd of the D♭ chord—a very consonant resolution. However, the other triplet notes are A and B♭, the ♯5 and 13, respectively, creating a mild dissonance. The last of the triplets (in measure 44) contain the dissonant ♭9 (A) and ♯5 (E) notes over the A♭7 chord, creating an A♭7♭9♯5 sound. The triplet motive is also alluded to in measures 62–63, leading to the end of the solo.

In measures 26–28, Django bends up a half step from E to F. Each time the bend occurs, however, it is displaced by half a beat, creating the illusion of a shifting beat. This acts as a catalyst for the bends in measures 29–32, where the E-to-F bend randomly starts on different beats throughout.

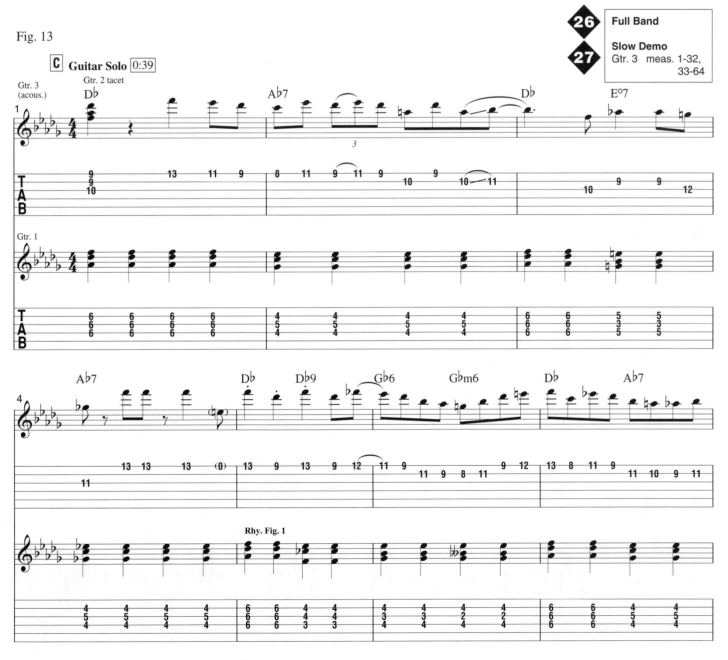

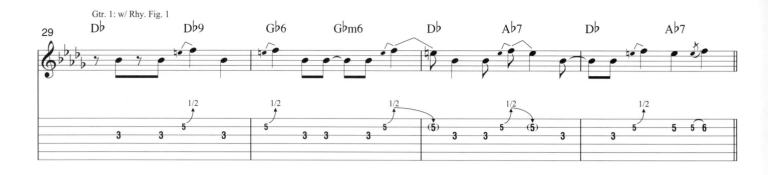

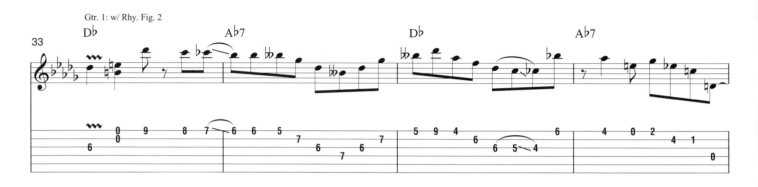

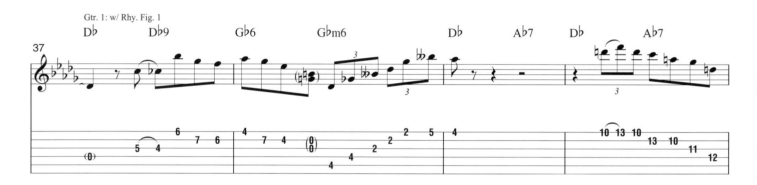

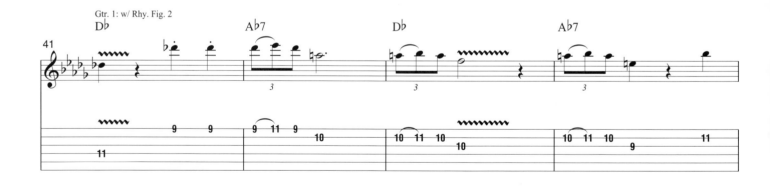

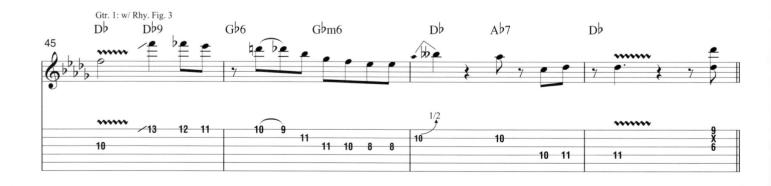

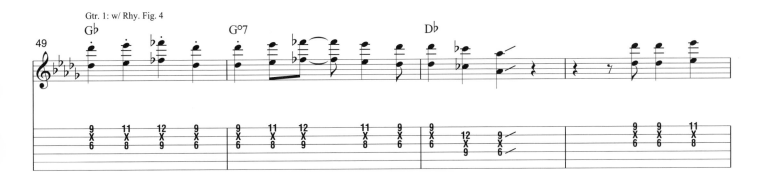

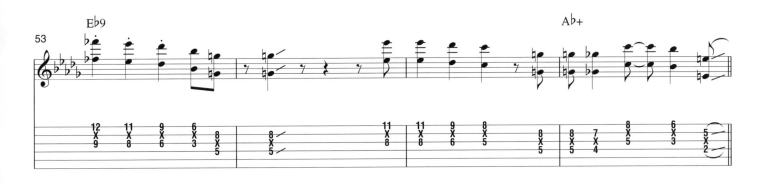

AIN'T MISBEHAVIN'

Words by Andy Razaf
Music by Thomas "Fats" Waller and Harry Brooks

Figure 14–Solo

Django Reinhardt's solo on "Ain't Misbehavin' ," with its motivic and rhythmic development, is an exemplary model of solo construction. After the opening quote of the theme, Django weaves through the chord changes with primarily scalar runs based on the D major scale (D–E–F♯–G–A–B–C♯). In measure 7 he introduces a triplet motive that is repeated for three consecutive measures. The motive begins on the root and hammers and pulls back and forth up a half step. This lick is transposed up a perfect 4th in measure 8 to correspond to the chord change (Bm–Em). In measure 9 the pattern begins on the 9th of the D chord and hammers onto the minor 3rd (F♮), creating a bluesy effect. Notice how the pattern gets rhythmically displaced in the following measures, starting on beat 3 in measure 7, beat 2 in measure 8, and back to beat 3 in measure 10. This figure is recalled in measures 39–40.

Another motive is introduced in measure 25, comprised of a note followed by a higher note, which is bent up a half step. Django leaps from A to E and bends up to F♮, the bluesy ♭3rd of the D chord. This is followed by a bend from G♯ to A, the 5th of the D chord. Some arpeggiated lines follow in measures 30–32, and in measures 33–36 Django continues to develop the bending motive, this time starting with a bend from E♯ to F♯, the 3rd of the D chord.

Chromaticism is abundant throughout the solo and used primarily in one of two ways: as neighbor tones and passing tones. For example, the triplet motive (mentioned above) in measures 7–9 uses a chromatic upper neighbor trill. In measure 58, chromatic passing tones fill the gap from A down to F♯. Measure 59 has an A♯ passing tone between A and B, measure 61 also has an A♯ passing tone between A and B (this time an octave lower), and in measure 62 there are chromatic passing tones from A♯ to C♯.

28 Full Band

29 Slow Demo
Gtr. 1 meas. 1-32, 33-49, 58-64

Fig. 14

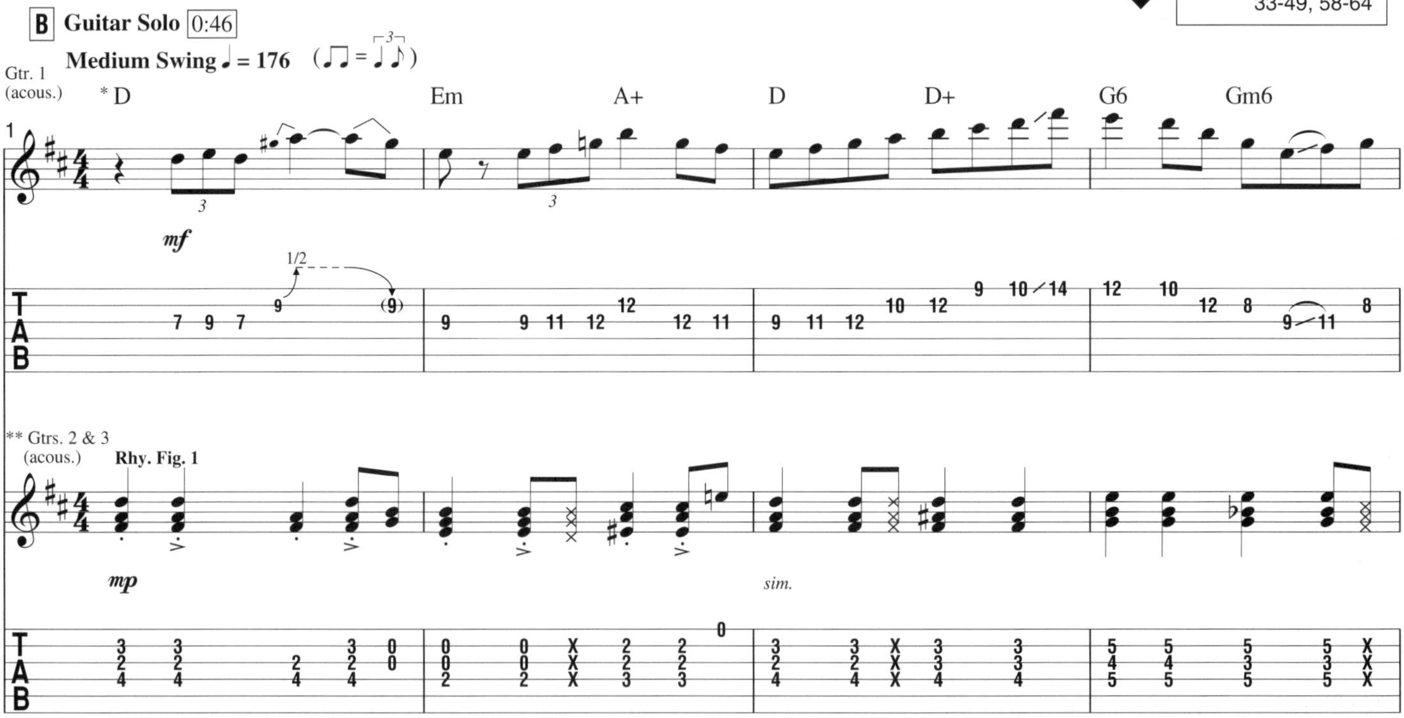

* Chord symbols reflect overall harmony.
** Composite arrangement

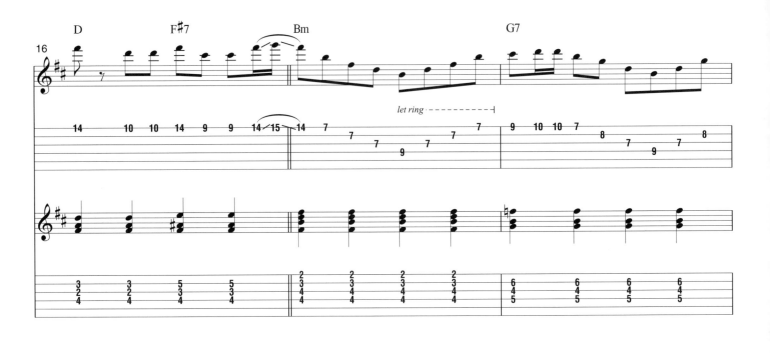

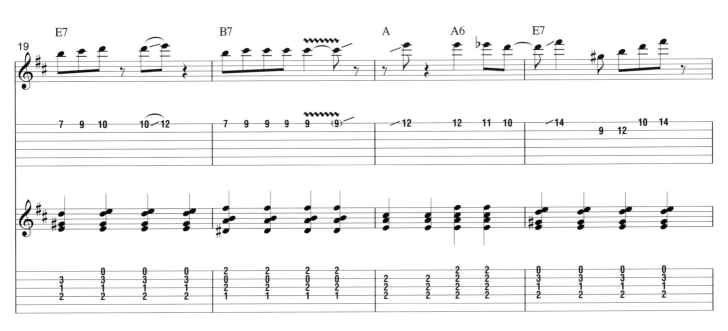

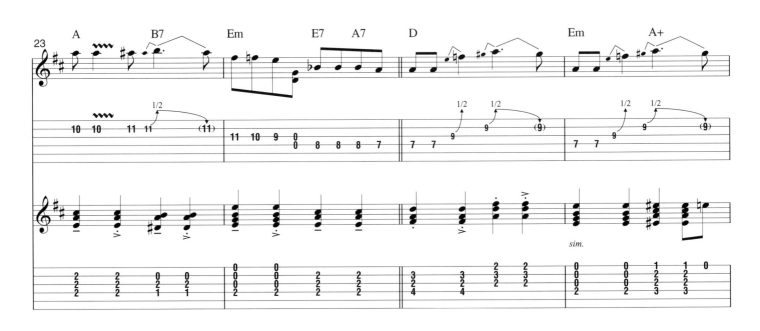

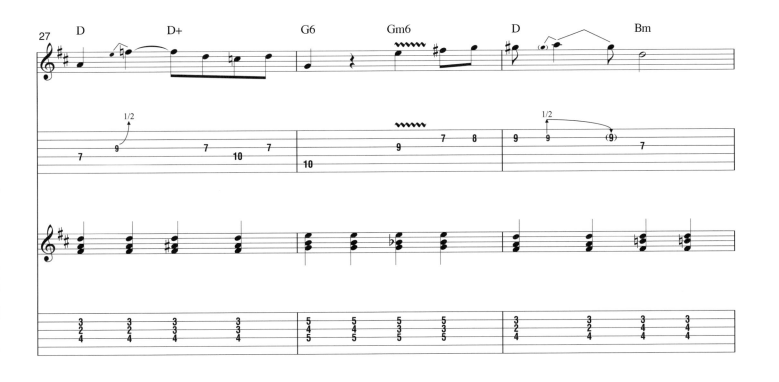

* Played ahead of the beat.

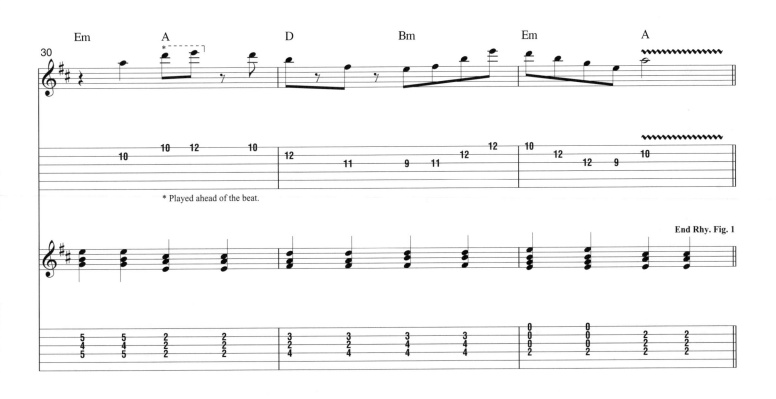

End Rhy. Fig. 1

Gtrs. 2 & 3: w/ Rhy. Fig. 1

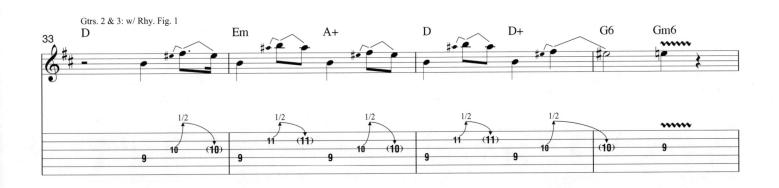

ROSE ROOM

Words by Harry Williams
Music by Art Hickman

Figure 15–Head and Solo

Five unaccompanied notes lead into the head of "Rose Room." Here, Django takes plenty of liberty with the melody playing unrelated, long, and intricate lines throughout. Chromatic passing tones are used to connect chord tones in measures 1–2, 7, 11–12, and 19. These tones can add momentum to a line and are a useful device in every jazz musician's arsenal.

Some of Django's lines contain interval leaps that connect lower notes to higher ones. In measure 32, there is a leap from G♯ to E, which requires string skipping to articulate, and in measures 37–38 there are leaps that connect the triplets with the quarter notes. Notice in measures 31–33 how the high notes ascend each time to create a melody of B–D–E in the high register. This "line within a line" approach is used again in measures 37–38, this time with the upper notes descending chromatically from F to D.

In measures 53–55, Django plays a chromatically descending trill pattern to lead into the A note, the 3rd of the F chord on the first beat of measure 55. A good lesson to learn from this is that you can play *anything* (even if it goes out of key) as long as it resolves into a definitive note. Django makes use of repeated notes in measures 15–16 and 25–26 to provide contrast against the multifarious lines. He concludes the solo with some pre-rock-era riffing in measures 62–65.

30 Full Band

31 Slow Demo
Gtr. 1 meas. 1-32,
33-64

Fig. 15

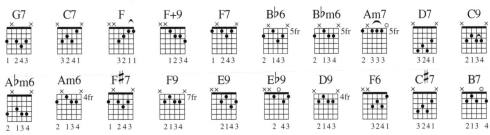

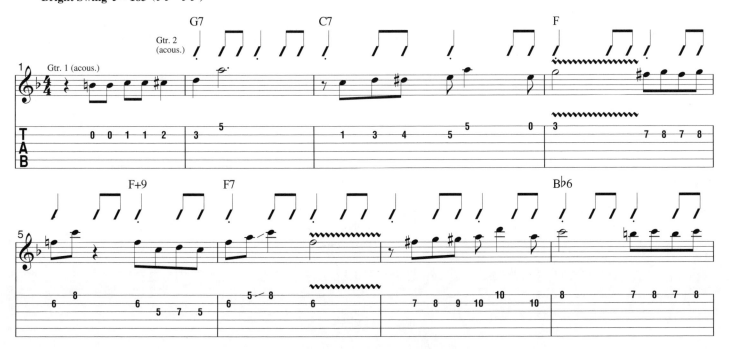

* trem. pick while sliding down

MINOR SWING

By Django Reinhardt and Stephane Grapelli

Figure 16–Intro

In the twelve-measure intro to "Minor Swing" the guitar and violin are unaccompanied and harmonize a simple melody played over a vamp of Am7 to Bm7♭5. The melody is based on chord tones and is harmonized primarily in 3rds. The duo lays out in measures 7–8 and a lone bass note fills in the gap. In measure 11, they lay out again, this time with a walking bass to fill in the space.

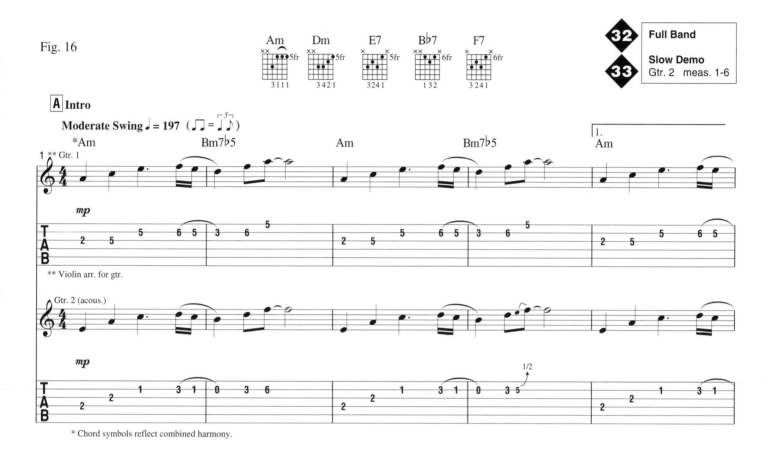

* Chord symbols reflect combined harmony.

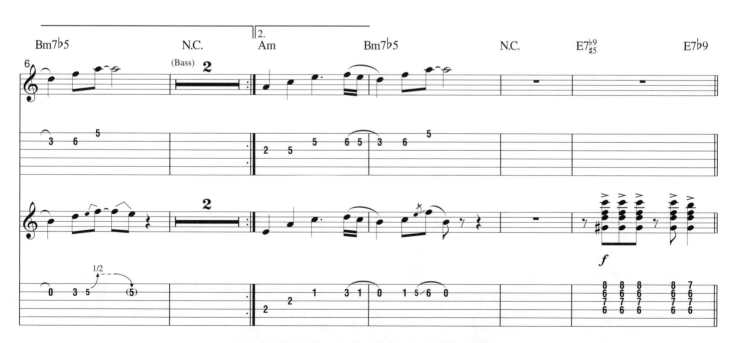

Figure 17–Head and Solo

The head to "Minor Swing" doesn't resemble a head in the conventional sense. It sounds more like an improvised section similar to some of the bebop heads written by jazz saxophone legend Charlie Parker. There is no detectable melody—rather an assortment of complex lines—and it's only played once at the beginning with no head out at the end.

There are many recurring themes in the head and solo, such as the use of an F°7 arpeggio (F–A♭(G♯)–B–D) over an E7 chord to create an E7♭9 sound in measures 5, 22, and 38. Another prominent figure is that of a chord tone approached by its lower and upper neighbor. This figure is heard in measures 2, 10, 13, 14, 19, 33, and 42.

Some nice rhythmic touches are heard in the syncopation of measures 8–9, which propels the music forward, and the barrage of eighth-note triplets in the chromatic scale passage of measures 52–54.

* Played behind the beat.

*T (5&6) = Thumb on 5th
& 6th strings

Figure 18–Outro

The sixteen-measure outro is reminiscent of the intro in its use of basic arpeggios over their corresponding chords. It starts off with an A minor arpeggio, like the intro, but then moves to a D minor chord rather than a Bm7♭5. The progression then proceeds to the dominant chord (E) and back to the tonic (Am). In measures 15–16 Django concludes the song with a stock ending played in octaves.

36 Full Band

37 Slow Demo
Gtr. 2   meas. 9-16

Fig. 18

61

DAPHNE
By Django Reinhardt

Figure 19–Head

"Daphne" is written with an AABA structure that is thirty-two measures long. The chord changes are similar to what jazz musicians call "rhythm changes" (changes from the George Gershwin classic "I Got Rhythm"). The difference here is the B section, which in "Daphne" is a I–VI–II–V progression in E♭, one half step higher than the key of D in the A section. Normally, a cycle of dominant chords is found in the B section of traditional "rhythm changes."

In this transcription, the violin melody is again arranged for guitar. To access the high notes in measures 2 and 4, shift from tenth position to twelfth position and use your pinky to hit the 17th fret. This is a stretch, but being so high up on the fretboard, it shouldn't pose a problem. In measures 9–11 there are several position shifts. Play the last three beats of measure 10 in fifth position and measures 11–12 in third position.

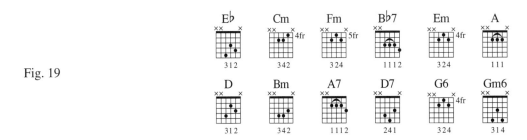

Fig. 19

* Chord symbols reflect overall harmony.
*** Composite arrangement

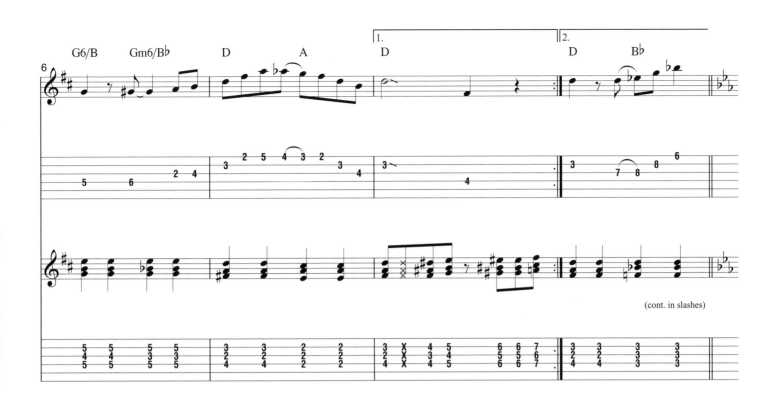

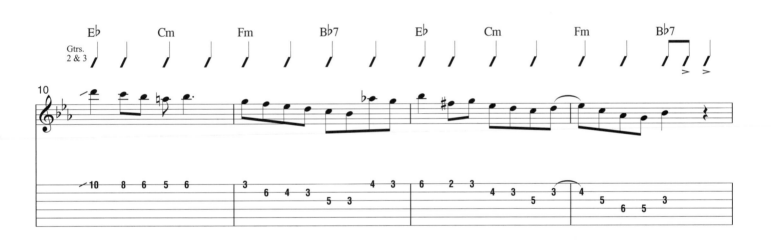

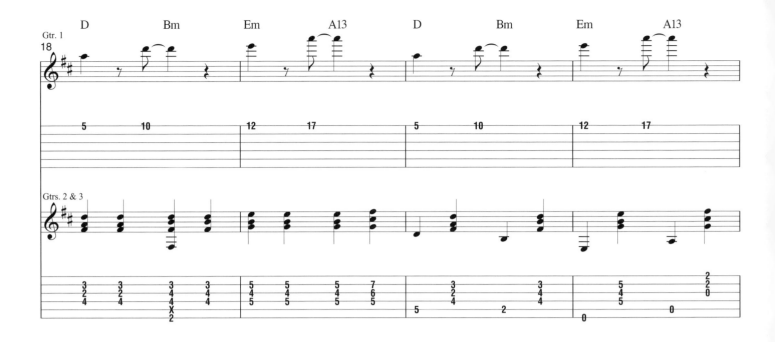

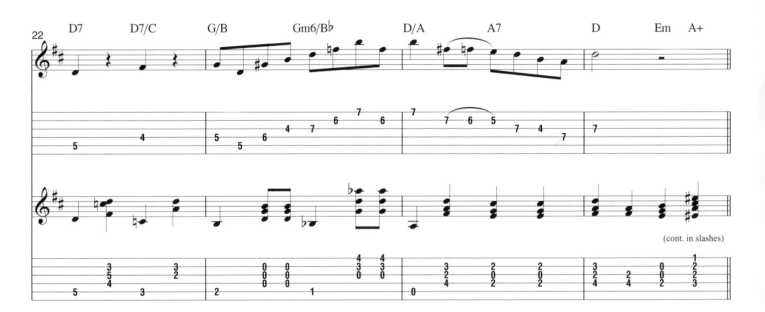

(cont. in slashes)

Figure 20 – Solo

In the solo to "Daphne," Django uses the rhythmic motive of starting a note on the "and" of beat one (influenced by the opening notes of the head) as a unifying factor for the first eight measures. Examine how, by playing a note a half-beat later, the accents shift to beat 2 and create a syncopated effect. The phrases in measures 1–3 utilize this rhythmic accenting, which leads to the phrase's conclusion in measure 4. In measure 5, Django starts off again with this rhythmic motive but uses it as a springboard to launch into a longer line that concludes on the downbeat of measure 9. This rhythmic motive is also heard in measures 13, 21, 27, 45, 47, 48, 58, 59, and 61.

Django makes use of the half-step bend, a staple of his improvising vocabulary. He rarely uses a whole step bend in his soloing and he typically bends into chord tones, as in measures 10, 45, and 63.

In measure 52 Django slips out of the key of E♭ to the key of E, a half step higher. This results in a pleasing dissonance that is resolved in the next measure. Jazz musicians use this technique of slide slipping to produce an "outside" effect and create color in their lines.

Fig. 20

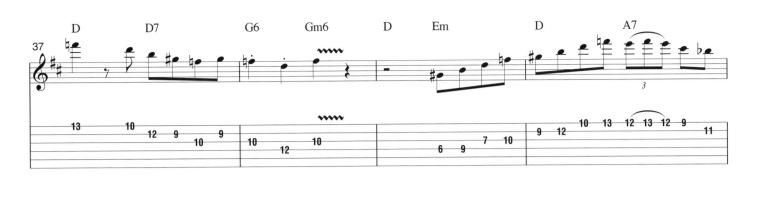

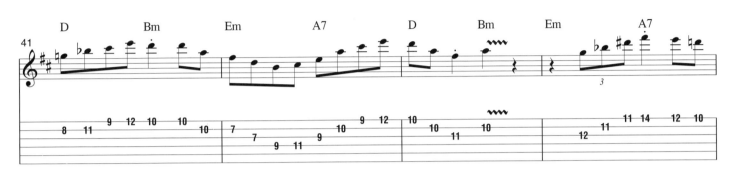

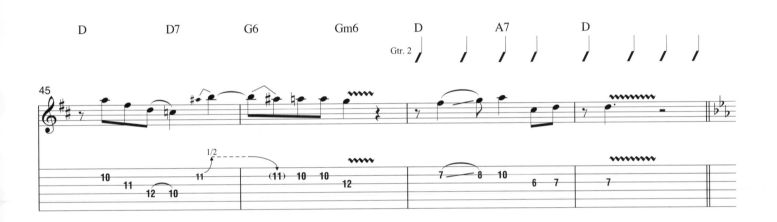

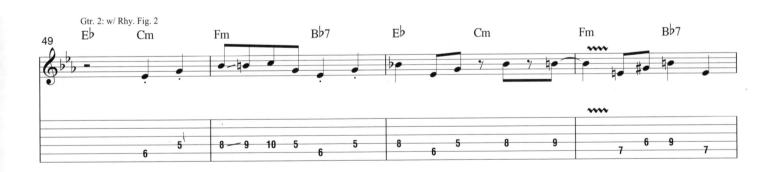

Figure 21 – Head Out

The final statement of the head foreshadows the innovations of jazz guitar legend Wes Montgomery. Here Django plays the head in octaves—a technique generally associated with Wes—doubled by the violin. To achieve a warm, round tone when playing octaves, use your right-hand thumb to strike the notes. Also be sure to dampen the inner string to prevent any unwanted string noise.

In measures 11–15, Django plays some arpeggiated runs, outlining the chords and their upper extensions—G and B♭, the 9th and 11th of F minor in measures 12 and 14, and A and D, the 6th and 9th of the C minor chord in measure 13. Django returns to more "Wes-like" figures, employing chord-melody passages in measures 16–18 with a return to octaves in measure 19.

42 Full Band

43 Slow Demo
Gtr. 3 meas. 1-15

Fig. 21

NUAGES

By Django Reinhardt and Jacques Larue

Figure 22–Solo

Django's "Nuages" is without a doubt his most famous composition. Countless musicians, including (surprisingly) forward-thinking fusion avatar Allan Holdsworth—on his 1996 release *None Too Soon*—have recorded it. It has stood the test of time and is now an essential part of the jazz repertoire.

In the solo to "Nuages" Django uses artificial harmonics to produce chiming melodies in measures 1–8. Artificial harmonics are typically created by playing a note (fretted or with an open string) while touching lightly over the fret wire with the index finger of the right hand twelve frets (one octave) higher, and plucking the string with either the right-hand thumb or a pick held by the thumb and middle finger. Seven-string guitarist Lenny Breau would later become famous for his use of artificial harmonics.

In measures 11–12 (beats 3–1), Django plays a lick similar to one that would later be popularized by bebop trumpeter Dizzy Gillespie and become a part of the jazz vernacular (commonly played at the end of a ballad over a tonic minor chord). This lick, based on the tonic minor chord (Dm), starts with the 5th of the chord (A) surrounded by its upper and lower neighbors, both a half step away. This is followed by a leap up to the ♭3rd (F), down to the 7th (C♯), and up to the 9th (E) resolving to the root.

A similar figure is heard in measures 14–15, with a D note embellished by its lower and upper neighbors. In measures 24–25, upper neighbors are used to precede the B♭ major chord tones. This leads into a fast B♭maj7 arpeggio that climbs from seventh position to the highest register of the guitar.

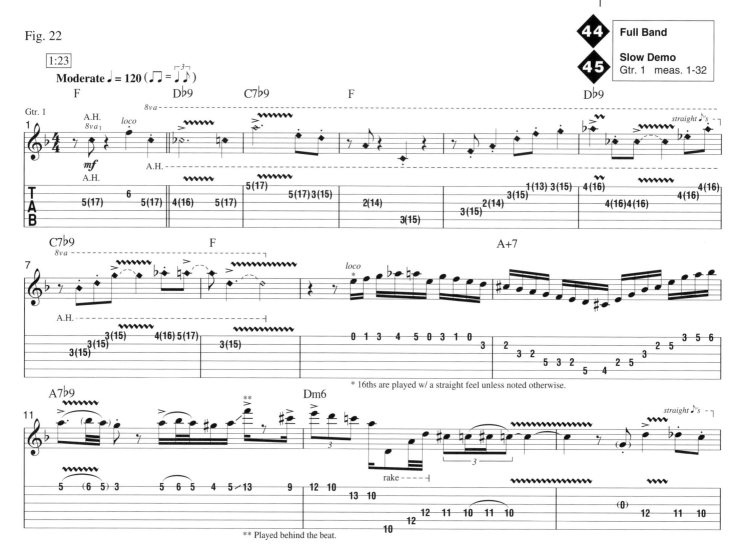

* 16ths are played w/ a straight feel unless noted otherwise.

** Played behind the beat.

SWING 42

By Django Reinhardt

Figure 23–Head

"Swing 42" is Django's dedication to jazz great Louis Armstrong. It is inspired by Armstrong's vocal melodies and most definitely swings. The A section's catchy riff is essentially based on a I–vi–ii–V progression with the melody spelling out the changes. The melody makes use of passing and leading tones to target chord and scale notes. For example, in measure 1–2, the G♯ passing tone is used to connect G (the ♭7 of Am7) to A (the 5th of Dm7). In measures 5–6 the G♯ passing tone resolves to A, the 5th of Dm7. These functional, chromatic approach notes are also heard in measures 3, 8, 9–10, 11, 13–14, 27, and 29–32.

After a quick modulation to the key of E, the B section starts off with a progression that clearly defines the key (much like the A section). A I–ii–V–I progression, the most common progression in jazz, is used exclusively here, sticking only to the key of E (except for the last chord, G7, which brings us back to C). This progression really hones in on the sound of the key and makes the modulation back to C stand out. Notice that the melody here is a very simple two-measure pattern that repeats over and over. There are no eighth-note lines, no chromaticism, and no virtuosic displays—just pure melody.

Throughout the head, a clarinet doubles the guitar to produce a round, bouncy sound that is appropriate for the song's playful melody. The A section melody is played primarily in fifth and seventh position with one position shift to fourth position in measures 8–9. By contrast, the B section is played in first position with the occasional use of open strings.

Fig. 23

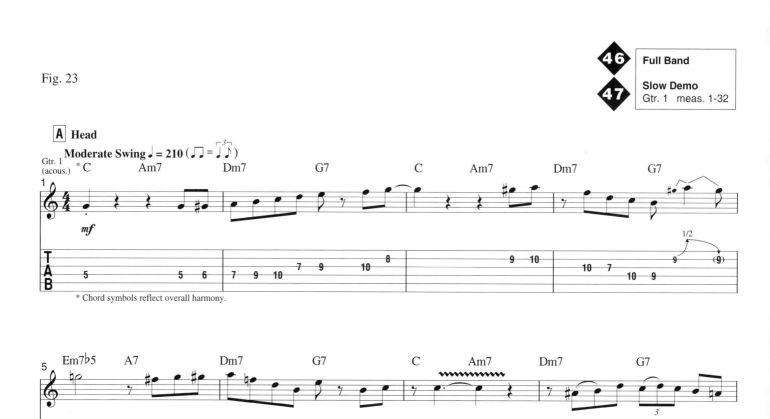

** T(6) = Thumb on 6th string

Figure 24–Solo

Django takes a compact one-chorus solo over this tune. For the first A section he plays it safe by playing primarily diatonic lines. There are some chromatic notes here and there, but he's going for a different approach that is more appropriate for the tune. In measures 9–12, Django uses the C minor pentatonic scale (C–E♭–F–G–B♭) with string bending and fast vibrato to add a bluesy touch.

For the B section, Django kicks it up a notch by introducing his long, wide-range, eighth-note lines. A particularly cool lick is the ascending E°7 arpeggio (E–G–B♭–C♯) in measure 20. Django plays this arpeggio using a two-notes-per-string approach, playing a minor 3rd finger shape that moves across the strings in tritones. Rock virtuosos Yngwie Malmsteen and the late Randy Rhoads would later adopt this diminished arpeggio shape.

For the last A section, Django whips out a hip lick in measures 25–26 that has a descending chromatic scale fragment interjected against a lower G pedal point. This lick has an almost atonal sound that is quickly assuaged by a grounded, earthy-sounding blues lick in measure 26–28. In measures 29–30, Django plays a line similar to his opening phrase in measures 1–2, but this time the line starts two beats earlier (on beat 2 as opposed to beat 4).

Fig. 24

48 Full Band

49 Slow Demo
Gtr. 1 meas. 1-32

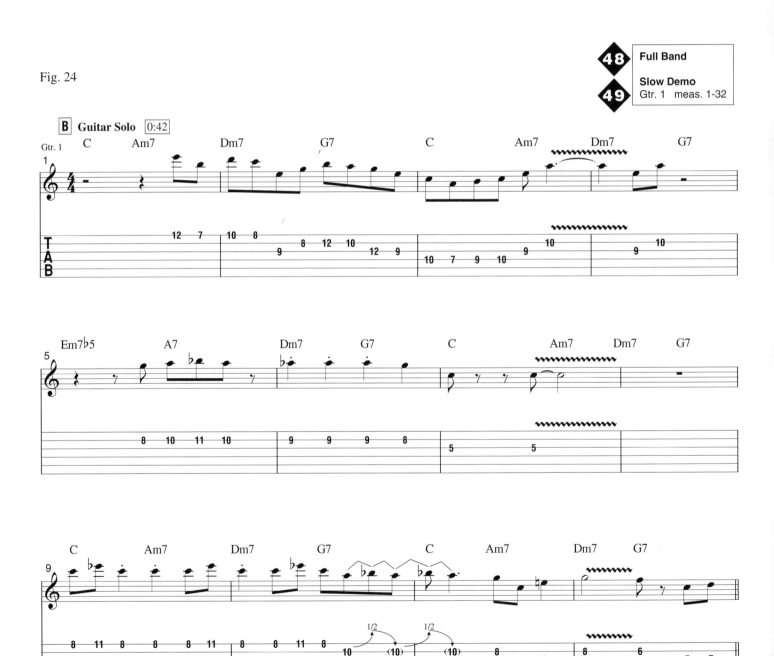

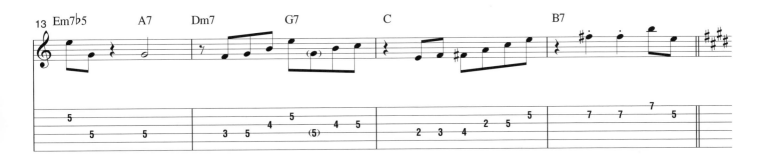

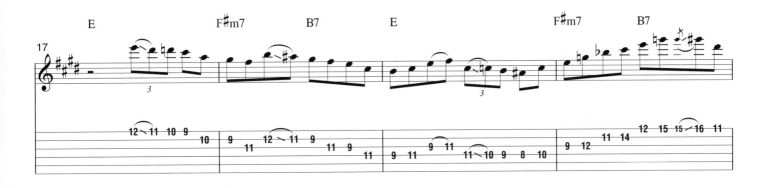

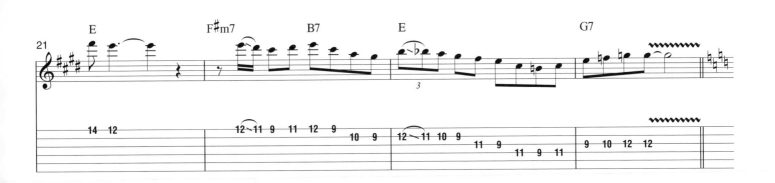

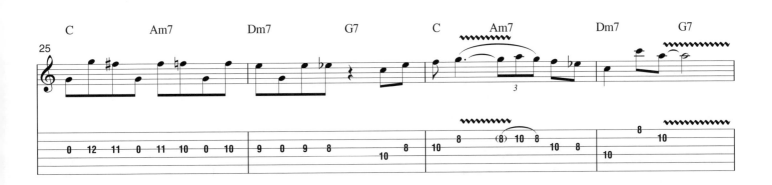

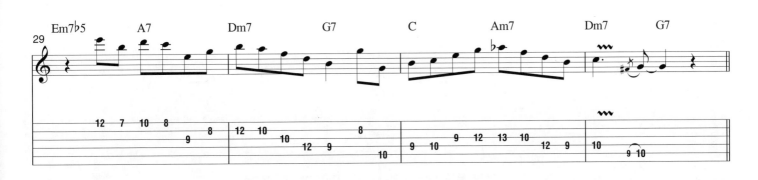

BELLEVILLE

By Django Reinhardt

Figure 25–Intro and Head

"Belleville" begins with guitar and clarinet trading licks, unaccompanied at a brisk tempo. Django's fast opening phrase is derived from the chromatic figure of the first two measures of the head (D–C♯–C♮–B). A quick arpeggiated descent outlining a D6 chord follows, and the clarinet enters (here transcribed for guitar). The clarinet line begins with an ascending figure that jumps to and descends chromatically from E. This line is also reminiscent of the chromatic line in the head.

"Belleville"'s head is thirty-two measures long with an AABA structure. The melody is based on a chromatic descent from the root of the tonic chord (D) to the 5th (A). Just before reaching the 5th, a G♯ is interjected to add to the urgency of resolution. The G♯ combined with the B♭ right before the A function as encircling tones—notes that surround a target note. This approach of encircling a target note became ubiquitous in the bebop and post-bop era and is now one of the tenets of contemporary jazz.

For the A section of the head, Django plays chords primarily in a quarter-note rhythm. This approach gives the music a sense of energy and makes the band swing. Here, Django overcomes his crippling disability by playing chords using the left-hand thumb to barre the fifth and sixth strings. Doing this also allowed him to sound out notes not playable with traditional left-hand technique; with this approach, Django was easily able to add colorful 6ths and 9ths to the chord voicing.

In the B section starting in measure 15, Django shifts gears and employs tremolo picking for the chords, creating a swishing sound. In measures 21–22 he returns to chord strumming, which leads into the final A section. In measures 26–27, amidst the comping, Django squeezes in some fast scalar passages.

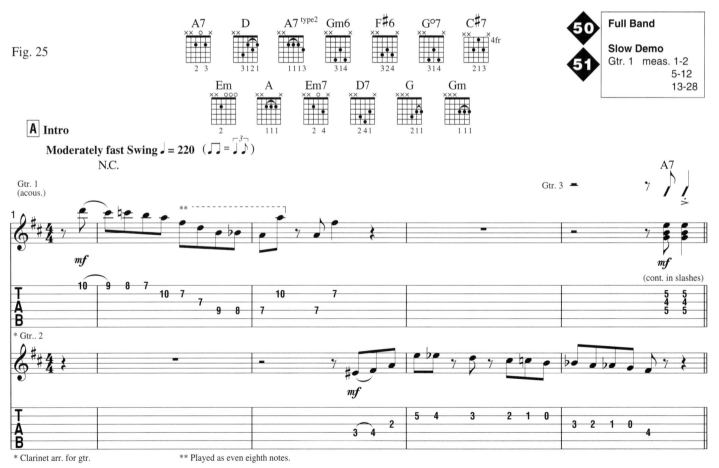

* Clarinet arr. for gtr.   ** Played as even eighth notes.

*** T (5&6) = Thumb on 5th & 6th strings

Figure 26–Solo

In the solo section, Django comes out in full force with the fire of a true madman. Arpeggios are employed throughout as in measures 3, 9–10, 13–14, and 17–19. The D° in measures 9–10 (beats 3–4) is interesting because it contains many notes that deny the tonality of the underlying D chord. Yet, since this arpeggio has such a strong sound, the result sounds polytonal (mixing more than one tonality at a time) rather than atonal. Here, the "wrong" notes sound right!

In measures 12–15, Django uses wide interval leaps. In measure 12 there is a leap down an octave, and in measures 13–14 there are two leaps up a 7th. Practice playing his section slowly at first, as the string skip to the higher note may pose a picking problem. Notice that Django leaps into the upper extensions of the chords, such as the 13th of the D chord and the 9th of the G chord.

For the final A section, Django winds down his solo by using fewer notes. Here he plays melodically and uses harmonics and bending to create a textural effect, which contrasts well with his fleet-fingered escapades.

Fig. 26

HONEYSUCKLE ROSE

Words by Andy Razaf
Music by Thomas "Fats" Waller

Figure 27–Head

Django takes a virtuosic approach to the swing classic "Honeysuckle Rose." The tempo is brisk, and Django weaves speedy eighth-note lines around the melody. In measure 13 he superimposes a B♭ minor pentatonic pattern over the C7 chord, creating hip altered notes such as the ♯9 (E♭) and ♭9 (D♭). In measure 62 he plays this lick again, this time displaced an eighth note earlier.

In measures 16–17, Django creates a rhythmic motive consisting of a single eighth note followed by an eighth-note rest. This catchy motive is recalled in measures 35–38 and morphs into an octave-and-fifth lick in measures 39–41. The motive is recalled again in measures 45–46.

Over the C7 chord in measures 28–29, Django plays a pattern of chromatic upper neighbor notes resolving down to the root (C) and 5th (G) by half steps. This phrase is manipulated rhythmically and creates an almost Bartokian effect.

Fig. 27

Figure 28–Solo

     The solo starts off with an attention-grabbing unison lick in the uppermost register of the guitar. The unison notes are played on adjacent strings and require a five-fret stretch—for Django, five frets between his first and second finger! After the unison lick he plays a bouncy lick on the twentieth fret before sliding out of this register.

     Some cool altered notes are played over the C7 chord in measures 10–13, reminiscent of a similar phrase played in the head. Here Django primarily uses quarter-note triplets to add rhythmic interest and distinguish the altered tones. The notes are derived primarily from the C altered dominant scale (C–Db–Eb–Fb–Gb–Ab–Bb), a scale that is an integral part of the jazz player's vernacular.

     More altered dominant madness is heard in measures 26–29, this time reminiscent of the Bartok lick from the head. Notice that the four-note cell (Db–C–Ab–G) in measure 26 is displaced to start a beat later in measure 27 and another beat later (this time playing the first two notes of the cell an octave lower) in measure 28.

Fig. 28

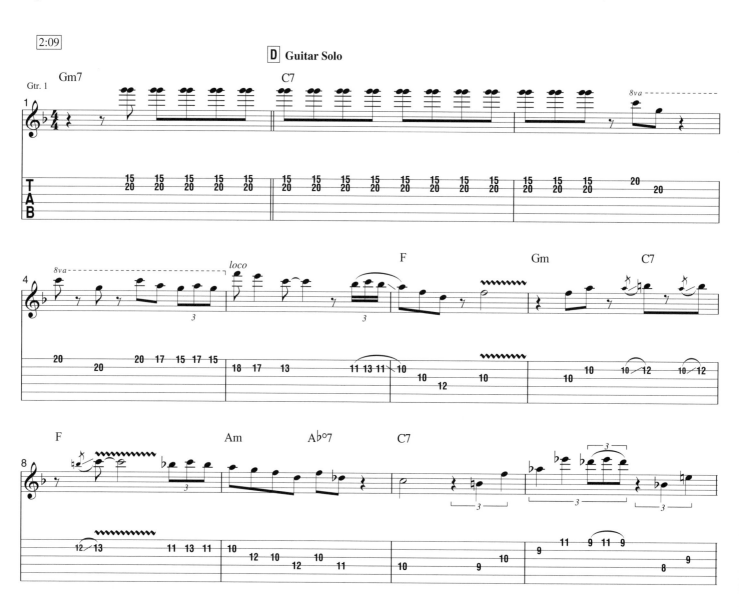

MARIE

Words and Music by Irving Berlin

Figure 29–Head

The head is written in a thirty-two-measure ABAB form with each section lasting for eight measures. The melody has a sanguine, lyrical quality that is suited for the violin (here arranged for guitar). At the B section (measures 9–16), the melody becomes more active both rhythmically and melodically—specifically in measures 13–16. In the second B section, starting from measure 29, the violin plays a string of eighth-note lines that are similar in content to Django's line playing.

Fig. 29

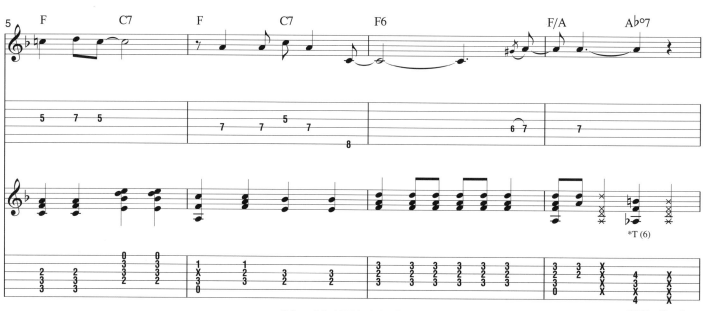

*T (6) = Thumb
on 6th string

* Played behind the beat.

sim.

let ring

Figure 30–Solo

Subtlety is not a characteristic trait of Django's soloing, and as soon as this solo starts he fires away with his signature long lines. The opening phrase in measures 1–2 outlines a Gm7 chord (G–B♭–D–F), which is here superimposed over a B♭ chord to create a colorful B♭6 sound. In measure 3, a B♭7 arpeggio is used to change the tonality to a dominant seventh sound. In measure 5 he plays an Fmaj7♯5 arpeggio (F–A–C♯–E) over the underlying F chord, taking advantage of the raised 5th (C♯) to create more tonal coloration.

Arpeggios are employed throughout the solo. In measures 26–27, a Gm7 arpeggio is used over its corresponding Gm7 chord, while in measure 29, over an F chord, an E°7 arpeggio (E–G–B♭–D♭) is played, implying a C7♭9 sound (the dominant chord of F). Django again also uses neighbor notes to lead into chord notes: in measure 17, an A lower-neighbor note precedes the tonic B♭ note; then, going into measure 18, diatonic upper-neighbor notes are used to fall into chord tones such as the E♭ landing into D, the G falling to F, and the C falling to B♭.

The four-measure breaks in measures 13–16 and 45–48 encapsulate Django's virtuosic style and add interest to the solo. He uses the F Locrian mode (F–G♭–A♭–B♭–C♭–D♭–E♭) in measures 45–48 to shape the sound of his line and to produce an altered sound over the dominant F chord. This contrasts with the primarily diatonic line based on the F major scale, used in the first break of measures 13–16. Django's rhythmic playing in measures 9–12, 49–52, and 57–59 also adds variety by breaking up his constant outpouring of notes. Subtle or not, this is a great solo.

60 Full Band

61 Slow Demo
Gtr. 1   meas. 1-32
33-64

Fig. 30

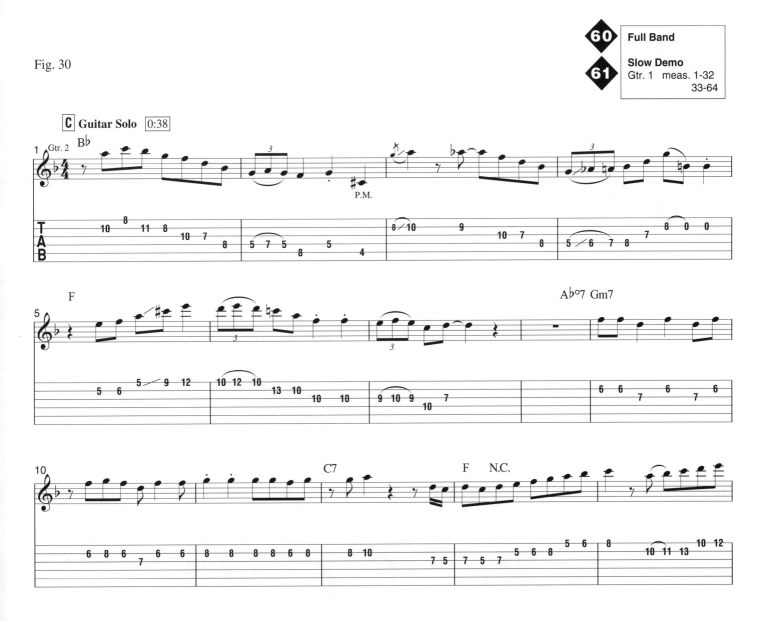

* Played behind the beat.

Guitar Notation Legend

Guitar Music can be notated three different ways: on a *musical staff*, in *tablature*, and in *rhythm slashes*.

RHYTHM SLASHES are written above the staff. Strum chords in the rhythm indicated. Use the chord diagrams found at the top of the first page of the transcription for the appropriate chord voicings. Round noteheads indicate single notes.

THE MUSICAL STAFF shows pitches and rhythms and is divided by bar lines into measures. Pitches are named after the first seven letters of the alphabet.

TABLATURE graphically represents the guitar fingerboard. Each horizontal line represents a a string, and each number represents a fret.

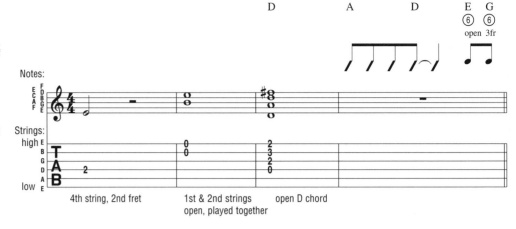

Definitions for Special Guitar Notation

HALF-STEP BEND: Strike the note and bend up 1/2 step.

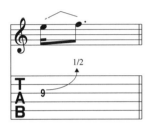

WHOLE-STEP BEND: Strike the note and bend up one step.

GRACE NOTE BEND: Strike the note and immediately bend up as indicated.

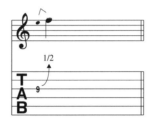

SLIGHT (MICROTONE) BEND: Strike the note and bend up 1/4 step.

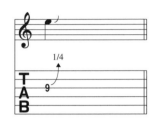

BEND AND RELEASE: Strike the note and bend up as indicated, then release back to the original note. Only the first note is struck.

PRE-BEND: Bend the note as indicated, then strike it.

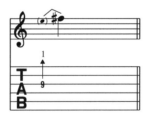

PRE-BEND AND RELEASE: Bend the note as indicated. Strike it and release the bend back to the original note.

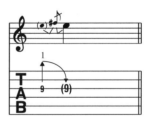

UNISON BEND: Strike the two notes simultaneously and bend the lower note up to the pitch of the higher.

VIBRATO: The string is vibrated by rapidly bending and releasing the note with the fretting hand.

WIDE VIBRATO: The pitch is varied to a greater degree by vibrating with the fretting hand.

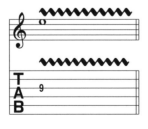

HAMMER-ON: Strike the first (lower) note with one finger, then sound the higher note (on the same string) with another finger by fretting it without picking.

PULL-OFF: Place both fingers on the notes to be sounded. Strike the first note and without picking, pull the finger off to sound the second (lower) note.

LEGATO SLIDE: Strike the first note and then slide the same fret-hand finger up or down to the second note. The second note is not struck.

SHIFT SLIDE: Same as legato slide, except the second note is struck.

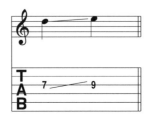

TRILL: Very rapidly alternate between the notes indicated by continuously hammering on and pulling off.

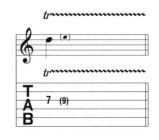

TAPPING: Hammer ("tap") the fret indicated with the pick-hand index or middle finger and pull off to the note fretted by the fret hand.

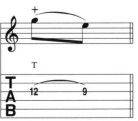

NATURAL HARMONIC: Strike the note while the fret-hand lightly touches the string directly over the fret indicated.

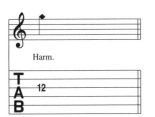

PINCH HARMONIC: The note is fretted normally and a harmonic is produced by adding the edge of the thumb or the tip of the index finger of the pick hand to the normal pick attack.

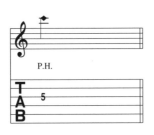

HARP HARMONIC: The note is fretted normally and a harmonic is produced by gently resting the pick hand's index finger directly above the indicated fret (in parentheses) while the pick hand's thumb or pick assists by plucking the appropriate string.

PICK SCRAPE: The edge of the pick is rubbed down (or up) the string, producing a scratchy sound.

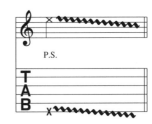

MUFFLED STRINGS: A percussive sound is produced by laying the fret hand across the string(s) without depressing, and striking them with the pick hand.

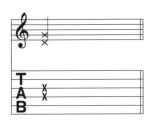

PALM MUTING: The note is partially muted by the pick hand lightly touching the string(s) just before the bridge.

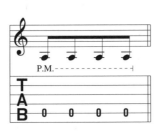

RAKE: Drag the pick across the strings indicated with a single motion.

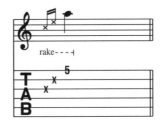

TREMOLO PICKING: The note is picked as rapidly and continuously as possible.

ARPEGGIATE: Play the notes of the chord indicated by quickly rolling them from bottom to top.

VIBRATO BAR DIVE AND RETURN: The pitch of the note or chord is dropped a specified number of steps (in rhythm) then returned to the original pitch.

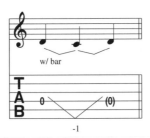

VIBRATO BAR SCOOP: Depress the bar just before striking the note, then quickly release the bar.

VIBRATO BAR DIP: Strike the note and then immediately drop a specified number of steps, then release back to the original pitch.

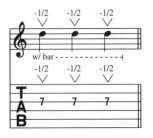

Additional Musical Definitions

 (accent) • Accentuate note (play it louder)

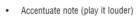 *(accent)* • Accentuate note with great intensity

 *(staccato)* • Play the note short

⊓ • Downstroke

∨ • Upstroke

D.S. al Coda • Go back to the sign (𝄋), then play until the measure marked "**To Coda**," then skip to the section labelled "**Coda**."

D.C. al Fine • Go back to the beginning of the song and play until the measure marked "**Fine**" (end).

Rhy. Fig. • Label used to recall a recurring accompaniment pattern (usually chordal).

Riff • Label used to recall composed, melodic lines (usually single notes) which recur.

Fill • Label used to identify a brief melodic figure which is to be inserted into the arrangement.

Rhy. Fill • A chordal version of a Fill.

tacet • Instrument is silent (drops out).

 • Repeat measures between signs.

 • When a repeated section has different endings, play the first ending only the first time and the second ending only the second time.

NOTE: Tablature numbers in parentheses mean:
1. The note is being sustained over a system (note in standard notation is tied), or
2. The note is sustained, but a new articulation (such as a hammer-on, pull-off, slide or vibrato begins), or
3. The note is a barely audible "ghost" note (note in standard notation is also in parentheses).

IMPROVE YOUR IMPROV

AND OTHER JAZZ TECHNIQUES WITH BOOKS FROM HAL LEONARD

JAZZ GUITAR
HAL LEONARD GUITAR METHOD
by Jeff Schroedl

The Hal Leonard Jazz Guitar Method is your complete guide to learning jazz guitar. This book uses real jazz songs to teach the basics of accompanying and improvising jazz guitar in the style of Wes Montgomery, Joe Pass, Tal Farlow, Charlie Christian, Pat Martino, Barney Kessel, Jim Hall, and many others.
00695359 Book/CD Pack.............................$14.95

AMAZING PHRASING
50 WAYS TO IMPROVE YOUR
IMPROVISATIONAL SKILLS • *by Tom Kolb*

This book/CD pack explores all the main components necessary for crafting well-balanced rhythmic and melodic phrases. It also explains how these phrases are put together to form cohesive solos. Many styles are covered – rock, blues, jazz, fusion, country, Latin, funk and more – and all of the concepts are backed up with musical examples.
00695583 Book/CD Pack.............................$16.95

BEST OF JAZZ GUITAR
by Wolf Marshall • Signature Licks

In this book/CD pack, Wolf Marshall provides a hands-on analysis of 10 of the most frequently played tunes in the jazz genre, as played by the leading guitarists of all time. Each selection includes technical analysis and performance notes, biographical sketches, and authentic matching audio with backing tracks.
00695586 Book/CD Pack.............................$24.95

CHORD-MELODY PHRASES FOR GUITAR
by Ron Eschete • REH ProLessons Series

Expand your chord-melody chops with these outstanding jazz phrases! This book covers: chord substitutions, chromatic movements, contrary motion, pedal tones, inner-voice movements, reharmonization techniques, and much more. Includes standard notation and tab, and a CD.
00695628 Book/CD Pack.............................$14.95

CHORDS FOR JAZZ GUITAR
THE COMPLETE GUIDE TO COMPING,
CHORD MELODY AND CHORD SOLOING • *by Charlton Johnson*

This book/CD pack will teach you how to play jazz chords all over the fretboard in a variety of styles and progressions. It covers: voicings, progressions, jazz chord theory, comping, chord melody, chord soloing, voice leading and many more topics. The CD includes 98 full-band demo tracks. No tablature.
00695706 Book/CD Pack.............................$19.95

CRASH COURSE ON JAZZ GUITAR VOICINGS
THE ESSENTIAL GUIDE FOR ALL GUITARISTS
by Hugh Burns • Artemis Editions

This ultimate beginner's guide to jazz guitar covers: jazz harmony explained simply, easy essential jazz shapes to get you playing right away, classic jazz progressions, vamps, turnarounds and substitutions and more.
00695815 Book/CD Pack.............................$9.95

FRETBOARD ROADMAPS – JAZZ GUITAR
THE ESSENTIAL GUITAR PATTERNS
THAT ALL THE PROS KNOW AND USE • *by Fred Sokolow*

This book/CD pack will get guitarists playing lead & rhythm anywhere on the fretboard, in any key! It teaches a variety of lead guitar styles using moveable patterns, double-note licks, sliding pentatonics and more, through easy-to-follow diagrams and instructions. The CD includes 54 full-demo tracks.
00695354 Book/CD Pack.............................$14.95

JAZZ IMPROVISATION FOR GUITAR
by Les Wise • REH ProLessons Series

This book/CD will allow you to make the transition from playing disjointed scales and arpeggios to playing melodic jazz solos that maintain continuity and interest for the listener. Topics covered include: tension and resolution, major scale, melodic minor scale, and harmonic minor scale patterns, common licks and substitution techniques, creating altered tension, and more! Features standard notation and tab, and a CD.
00695657 Book/CD Pack.............................$16.95

JAZZ RHYTHM GUITAR
THE COMPLETE GUIDE
by Jack Grassel

This book/CD pack will help rhythm guitarists better understand: chord symbols and voicings, comping styles and patterns, equipment, accessories and set-up, the fingerboard, chord theory, and much more. The accompanying CD includes 74 full-band tracks.
00695654 Book/CD Pack.............................$19.95

JAZZ SOLOS FOR GUITAR
LEAD GUITAR IN THE STYLES OF TAL FARLOW,
BARNEY KESSEL, WES MONTGOMERY, JOE PASS, JOHNNY SMITH
by Les Wise

Examine the solo concepts of the masters with this book including phrase-by-phrase performance notes, tips on arpeggio substitution, scale substitution, tension and resolution, jazz-blues, chord soloing, and more. The CD includes full demonstration and rhythm-only tracks.
00695447 Book/CD Pack.............................$17.95

101 MUST-KNOW JAZZ LICKS
A QUICK, EASY REFERENCE GUIDE
FOR ALL GUITARISTS • *by Wolf Marshall*

Here are 101 definitive licks, plus a demonstration CD, from every major jazz guitar style, neatly organized into easy-to-use categories. They're all here: swing and pre-bop, bebop, post-bop modern jazz, hard bop and cool jazz, modal jazz, soul jazz and postmodern jazz. Includes an introduction, tips for using the book/CD, and a list of suggested recordings.
00695433 Book/CD Pack.............................$16.95

SWING AND BIG BAND GUITAR
FOUR-TO-THE-BAR COMPING IN THE STYLE OF
FREDDIE GREEN • *by Charlton Johnson*

This unique package teaches the essentials of swing and big band styles, including chord voicings, inversions, substitutions; time and groove, reading charts, chord reduction, and expansion; sample songs, patterns, progressions, and exercises; chord reference library; and a CD with over 50 full-demo examples. Uses chord grids – no tablature.
00695147 Book/CD Pack $16.95

PLAY THE CLASSICS
JAZZ FOLIOS FOR GUITARISTS

BEST OF JAZZ GUITAR
by Wolf Marshall • Signature Licks

INCLUDES TAB

In this book/CD pack, Wolf Marshall provides a hands-on analysis of 10 of the most frequently played tunes in the jazz genre, as played by the leading guitarists of all time. Features: All the Things You Are • How Insensitive • I'll Remember April • So What • Yesterdays • and more.
00695586 Book/CD Pack......................................$24.95

50 ESSENTIAL BEBOP HEADS ARRANGED FOR GUITAR
INCLUDES TAB

The best lines of Charlie Parker, Dizzy Gillespie, Thelonious Monk, and many more, for guitar with notes and tab. Includes: Donna Lee • Groovin' High • Ornithology • Confirmation • Epistrophy • and more.
00698990 ....$14.95

GUITAR STANDARDS
Classic Jazz Masters Series

INCLUDES TAB

16 classic jazz guitar performances transcribed note for note with tablature: All of You (Kenny Burrell) • Easter Parade (Herb Ellis) • I'll Remember April (Grant Green) • Lover Man (Django Reinhardt) • Song for My Father (George Benson) • The Way You Look Tonight (Wes Montgomery) • and more. Includes a discography.
00699143 Guitar Transcriptions $14.95

JAZZ BALLADS FOR FINGERSTYLE GUITAR
INCLUDES TAB

21 standards, including: Cry Me a River • Easy to Love • In a Sentimental Mood • Isn't It Romantic? • Mood Indigo • My Funny Valentine • My Romance • Some Enchanted Evening • Stella by Starlight • The Way You Look Tonight • When I Fall in Love • and more.
00699028 Fingerstyle Guitar $12.95

JAZZ CLASSICS FOR SOLO GUITAR
arranged by Robert B. Yelin

INCLUDES TAB

This collection includes excellent chord melody arrangements in standard notation and tablature for 35 all-time jazz favorites: April in Paris • Cry Me a River • Day by Day • God Bless' the Child • It Might as Well Be Spring • Lover • My Romance • Nuages • Satin Doll • Tenderly • Unchained Melody • Wave • and more!
00699279 Solo Guitar $17.95

JAZZ FAVORITES FOR SOLO GUITAR
arranged by Robert B. Yelin

INCLUDES TAB

This fantastic 35-song collection includes lush chord melody arrangements in standard notation and tab: Autumn in New York • Call Me Irresponsible • How Deep Is the Ocean • I Could Write a Book • The Lady Is a Tramp • Mood Indigo • Polka Dots and Moonbeams • Solitude • Take the "A" Train • Where or When • more.
00699278 Solo Guitar $17.95

JAZZ GEMS FOR SOLO GUITAR
arranged by Robert B. Yelin

INCLUDES TAB

35 great solo arrangements of jazz classics, including: After You've Gone • Alice in Wonderland • The Christmas Song • Four • Meditation • Stompin' at the Savoy • Sweet and Lovely • Waltz for Debby • Yardbird Suite • You'll Never Walk Alone • You've Changed • and more.
00699617 Solo Guitar $17.95

JAZZ GUITAR BIBLE
INCLUDES TAB

The one book that has all of the jazz guitar classics transcribed note-for-note, with standard notation and tablature. Includes over 30 songs: Body and Soul • Girl Talk • I'll Remember April • In a Sentimental Mood • My Funny Valentine • Nuages • Satin Doll • So What • Stardust • Take Five • Tangerine • Yardbird Suite • and more.
00690466 Guitar Recorded Versions $19.95

JAZZ GUITAR CHORD MELODIES
arranged & performed by Dan Towey

INCLUDES TAB

This book/CD pack includes complete solo performances of 12 standards, including: All the Things You Are • Body and Soul • My Romance • How Insensitive • My One and Only Love • and more. The arrangements are performance level and range in difficulty from intermediate to advanced.
00698988 Book/CD Pack $19.95

JAZZ GUITAR PLAY-ALONG
Guitar Play-Along Volume 16

INCLUDES TAB

With this book/CD pack, all you have to do is follow the tab, listen to the CD to hear how the guitar should sound, and then play along using the separate backing tracks. 8 songs: All Blues • Bluesette • Footprints • How Insensitive (Insensatez) • Misty • Satin Doll • Stella by Starlight • Tenor Madness.
00699584 Book/CD Pack $12.95

THE JAZZ STANDARDS BOOK

106 fantastic standards in easy guitar format (without tablature). Songs include: Ain't Misbehavin' • Blue Skies • Come Rain or Come Shine • Fly Me to the Moon • Georgia on My Mind • How High the Moon • It Don't Mean a Thing (If It Ain't Got That Swing) • My Romance • Slightly Out of Tune • Tangerine • and more.
00702164 Easy Guitar $15.95

JAZZ STANDARDS FOR FINGERSTYLE GUITAR
INCLUDES TAB

20 songs, including: All the Things You Are • Autumn Leaves • Bluesette • Body and Soul • Fly Me to the Moon • The Girl from Ipanema • How Insensitive • I've Grown Accustomed to Her Face • My Funny Valentine • Satin Doll • Stompin' at the Savoy • and more.
00699029 Fingerstyle Guitar $10.95

JAZZ STANDARDS FOR SOLO GUITAR
arranged by Robert B. Yelin

INCLUDES TAB

35 chord melody guitar arrangements, including: Ain't Misbehavin' • Autumn Leaves • Bewitched • Cherokee • Darn That Dream • Girl Talk • I've Got You Under My Skin • Lullaby of Birdland • My Funny Valentine • A Nightingale Sang in Berkeley Square • Stella by Starlight • The Very Thought of You • and more.
00699277 Solo Guitar $17.95

Prices, contents and availability subject to change without notice.

0805

ARTIST TRANSCRIPTIONS®

Artist Transcriptions are authentic, note-for-note transcriptions of the hottest artists in jazz, pop, and rock today. These outstanding, accurate arrangements are in an easy-to-read format which includes all essential lines. Artist Transcriptions can be used to perform, sequence or reference.

GUITAR & BASS

George Benson
00660113 Guitar Style of $14.95

Pierre Bensusan
00699072 Guitar Book of.................$19.95

Ron Carter
00672331 Acoustic Bass.................$16.95

Stanley Clarke
00672307 The Collection.................$19.95

Al Di Meola
00604041 Cielo E Terra $14.95
00660115 Friday Night in
San Francisco..............$14.95
00604043 Music, Words, Pictures....$14.95

Tal Farlow
00673245 Jazz Style of $19.95

Bela Fleck and the Flecktones
00672359 Melody/Lyrics/Chords......$18.95

Frank Gambale
00672336 Best of $22.95

Jim Hall
00699389 Jazz Guitar Environments ..$19.95
00699306 Exploring Jazz Guitar $17.95

Allan Holdsworth
00604049 Reaching for the
Uncommon Chord $14.95

Leo Kottke
00699215 Eight Songs $14.95

Wes Montgomery
00675536 Guitar Transcriptions $17.95

Joe Pass
00672353 The Collection.................$18.95

John Patitucci
00673216 ....$14.95

Django Reinhardt
00027083 Anthology $14.95
00026711 The Genius of $10.95
00026715 A Treasury of Songs $12.95

Johnny Smith
00672374 Guitar Solos $16.95

Mike Stern
00673224 Guitar Book.....................$16.95

Mark Whitfield
00672320 Guitar Collection..............$19.95

Gary Willis
00672337 The Collection.................$19.95

SAXOPHONE

Julian "Cannonball" Adderley
00673244 The Collection.................$19.95

Michael Brecker
00673237 ....$19.95
00672429 The Collection.................$19.95

The Brecker Brothers
00672351 And All Their Jazz............$19.95
00672447 Best of $19.95

Benny Carter
00672314 The Collection.................$22.95
00672315 Plays Standards $22.95

James Carter
00672394 The Collection.................$19.95

John Coltrane
00672494 A Love Supreme..............$12.95
00672529 Giant Steps.....................$14.95
00672493 Plays Coltrane Changes..$19.95
00672349 Plays Giant Steps $19.95
00672453 Plays Standards $19.95
00673233 Solos...............................$22.95

Paul Desmond
00672328 The Collection.................$19.95
00672454 Standard Time $19.95

Kenny Garrett
00672530 The Collection.................$19.95

Stan Getz
00699375 ....$18.95
00672377 Bossa Novas $19.95
00672375 Standards $17.95

Coleman Hawkins
00672523 The Collection.................$19.95

Joe Henderson
00672330 Best of $22.95
00673252 Selections from Lush Life
& So Near So Far $19.95

Kenny G
00673239 Best of $19.95
00673229 Breathless......................$19.95
00672462 Classics in the Key of G ..$19.95
00672485 Faith: A Holiday Album....$14.95
00672373 The Moment $19.95
00672516 Paradise $14.95

Joe Lovano
00672326 The Collection.................$19.95

Jackie McLean
00672498 The Collection.................$19.95

James Moody
00672372 The Collection $19.95

Frank Morgan
00672416 The Collection.................$19.95

Sonny Rollins
00672444 The Collection.................$19.95

David Sanborn
00675000 The Collection.................$16.95

Bud Shank
00672528 The Collection.................$19.95

Wayne Shorter
00672498 New Best of $19.95

Lew Tabackin
00672455 The Collection.................$19.95

Stanley Turrentine
00672334 The Collection.................$19.95

Lester Young
00672524 The Collection.................$19.95

PIANO & KEYBOARD

Monty Alexander
00672338 The Collection.................$19.95
00672487 Plays Standards $19.95

Kenny Barron
00672318 The Collection.................$22.95

Count Basie
00672520 The Collection.................$19.95

Warren Bernhardt
00672364 The Collection.................$19.95

Cyrus Chesnut
00672439 The Collection.................$19.95

Billy Childs
00673242 The Collection.................$19.95

Chick Corea
00672300 Paint the World $12.95

Bill Evans
00672537 At Town Hall $16.95
00672365 The Collection.................$19.95
00672425 Piano Interpretations.......$19.95
00672510 Trio, Vol. 1: 1959-1961 ...$24.95
00672511 Trio, Vol. 2: 1962-1965 ....$24.95
00672512 Trio, Vol. 3: 1968-1974 ....$24.95
00672513 Trio, Vol. 4: 1979-1980 ....$24.95

Benny Goodman
00672492 The Collection.................$16.95

Benny Green
00672329 The Collection.................$19.95

Vince Guaraldi
00672486 The Collection.................$19.95

Herbie Hancock
00672419 The Collection.................$19.95

Gene Harris
00672446 The Collection.................$19.95

Hampton Hawes
00672438 The Collection.................$19.95

Ahmad Jamal
00672322 The Collection.................$22.95

CLARINET

Buddy De Franco
00672423 The Collection.................$19.95

FLUTE

Eric Dolphy
00672379 The Collection.................$19.95

James Moody
00672372 The Collection $19.95

James Newton
00660108 Improvising Flute $14.95

Lew Tabackin
00672455 The Collection.................$19.95

TROMBONE

J.J. Johnson
00672332 The Collection.................$19.95

Brad Mehldau
00672476 The Collection.................$19.95

Thelonious Monk
00672388 Best of $19.95
00672389 The Collection.................$19.95
00672390 Jazz Standards, Vol. 1 ....$19.95
00672391 Jazz Standards, Vol. 2 ....$19.95
00672392 Intermediate Piano Solos..$14.95

Jelly Roll Morton
00672433 The Piano Rolls...............$12.95

Oscar Peterson
00672531 Plays Duke Ellington........$19.95
00672534 Very Best of $19.95

Michael Petrucciani
00673226 ....$17.95

Bud Powell
00672371 Classics $19.95
00672376 The Collection.................$19.95

André Previn
00672437 The Collection.................$19.95

Gonzalo Rubalcaba
00672507 The Collection.................$19.95

Horace Silver
00672303 The Collection.................$19.95

Art Tatum
00672316 The Collection.................$22.95
00672355 Solo Book $19.95

Billy Taylor
00672357 The Collection.................$24.95

McCoy Tyner
00673215 ....$16.95

Cedar Walton
00672321 The Collection.................$19.95

Kenny Werner
00672519 The Collection.................$19.95

Teddy Wilson
00672434 The Collection.................$19.95

TRUMPET

Louis Armstrong
00672480 The Collection.................$14.95
00672481 Plays Standards $14.95

Chet Baker
00672435 The Collection.................$19.95

Randy Brecker
00673234 ....$17.95

The Brecker Brothers
00672351 And All Their Jazz............$19.95
00672447 Best of $19.95

Miles Davis
00672448 Originals, Vol. 1 ....$19.95
00672451 Originals, Vol. 2 ....$19.95
00672450 Standards, Vol. 1 ....$19.95
00672449 Standards, Vol. 2 ....$19.95

Dizzy Gillespie
00672479 The Collection.................$19.95

Freddie Hubbard
00673214 ....$14.95

Tom Harrell
00672382 Jazz Trumpet Solos $19.95

Chuck Mangione
00672506 The Collection.................$19.95

FOR MORE INFORMATION, SEE YOUR LOCAL MUSIC DEALER,
OR WRITE TO:

HAL•LEONARD®
CORPORATION

7777 W. BLUEMOUND RD. P.O. BOX 13819 MILWAUKEE, WI 53213

Visit our web site for a complete listing
of our titles with songlists at
www.halleonard.com

Prices and availability subject to change without notice.

0105